The Strategic Use of Referendums

The Strategic Use of Referendums: Power, Legitimacy, and Democracy

Mark Clarence Walker

First published 2003 by
PALGRAVE MACMILLAN™
175 Fifth Avenue, New York, N.Y. 10010 and
Houndmills, Basingstoke, Hampshire, England RG21 6XS
Companies and representatives throughout the world.

PALGRAVE MACMILLAN is the global academic imprint of the Palgrave Macmillan division of St. Martin's Press, LLC and of Palgrave Macmillan Ltd. Macmillan® is a registered trademark in the United States, United Kingdom and other countries. Palgrave is a registered trademark in the European Union and other countries.

ISBN 1–4039–6263–4 hardback

Library of Congress Cataloging-in-Publication Data
Walker, Mark Clarence.
    The strategic use of referendums : power, legitimacy, and democracy/ by Mark Clarence Walker.
        p. cm.
    Includes bibliographical references and index.
    ISBN 1–4039–6263–4
    1. Referendum. 2. Power (Social sciences). 3. Legitimacy of governments. 4. Democracy. I. Title.

JF491.W35 2003
328.23'3—dc21   2003048670

A catalogue record for this book is available from the British Library.

Design by Newgen Imaging Systems (P) Ltd., Chennai, India.

First edition: August, 2003
10 9 8 7 6 5 4 3 2 1

Printed in the United States of America.

For my parents
Walter and Sarah

Table of Contents

Preface   ix

Chapter 1   **Legitimacy, Bargaining, and Power in
                the Use of Referendums**   1

Chapter 2   **Referendums and Executives in France and
                Chile**   19

Chapter 3   **The USSR Referendum and Republic
                Counter-Referendums**   49

Chapter 4   **Bargaining and Power in Russian Referendums**   73

Chapter 5   **Patterns in the Use of Referendums**   91

Chapter 6   **Pros and Cons of Referendums and
                Democratic Theory**   117

Notes   135

Bibliography   145

Index   155

Preface

The research for this study includes primary and secondary source material on the French referendums under de Gaulle, several Chilean referendums in the 1970s and 1980s, and the entire set of Soviet and Post-Soviet referendums—at the federal, republic, and local levels—from 1990 through 1997. Sources were collected in Russian, French, Spanish, and English, and included official government reports, newspaper articles, television and radio stories, academic articles and books, and a few interviews. Extensive time was spent in archives in Moscow as well as the University of California at Berkeley, the Hoover Institute at Stanford University, various locations in Washington, D.C., and on the Internet. Special thanks should be given to the Foreign Broadcast Information Service (FBIS), Radio Free Europe and Radio Liberty (RFE/RL), and the Open Media Research Institute (OMRI). I often began with their work as a starting point and rarely was their information found to be inaccurate.

This research has been supported over the years by a variety of sources. I have received support from the Institute for the Study of World Politics (the Dorothy Danforth Compton fellowship), American University (the Junior Faculty Teaching Release fellowship), and numerous grants from the Berkeley Program in Soviet and Post-Soviet Studies and the Department of Political Science at the University of California at Berkeley. I am especially proud of being a recipient of the David Bell Memorial Fellowship from the political science department at Berkeley. I knew David all too briefly; I can only hope that I have sufficiently honored his memory.

The following individuals played a significant role in my intellectual development and the success of this project, but none more so than Henry E. Brady and George W. Breslauer. Many thanks also go to Bruce Cain, Robert Powell, Peter Ordeshook, Robert Bates, Philip Roeder, Karen Dawisha, Joe Oppenheimer, Louis Goodman, Nanette Levinson, and, without a doubt, to David Pervin, my editor at Palgrave.

My spouse, Angela, played a central and irreplaceable role in the completion of this project. As my partner she provided me strength on countless occasions when I had little of my own. As an advisor she provided effective organizational tips for my daily work habits and unforgiving editing skills toward earlier drafts of this document. Much of my inspiration to complete and revise this manuscript came from her.

My greatest thanks go to the two most important teachers in my life, my parents—Walter C. Walker and Sarah E. Walker. How could I ignore the singular source of motivation to complete this project when asked, "Haven't you finished that book report yet?" Throughout this process my parents have supported me, emotionally and financially, without question. I owe them everything, of course, and thus this work is dedicated to them.

CHAPTER 1

Legitimacy, Bargaining, and Power in the Use of Referendums

Political actors use referendums to achieve their goals.[1] They do so deliberately and sometimes manipulatively with respect to the general public. Though the technical rules for the use of this device differ from state to state, actors recognize the referendum—a submission of a proposed public measure or actual statute to a direct popular vote— as one way and perhaps at times the best way to resolve an issue in their favor. Democratic governance demands a degree of compromise between actors like presidents, prime ministers, governors, and legislators of all types. But not all actors at all times settle for what a system based upon compromise provides. A referendum can then be introduced to allow for a different outcome more to the liking of the actor who proposed it.

Actors in nondemocratic states have used referendums for the same purpose. Indeed, authoritarian states have developed a fondness for referendums because they grant legitimacy to a policy position and the implementers of the device by utilizing the vote of the people.[2] In political systems short of legitimacy these votes have had profound effects: the establishment of presidential regimes, state secessions from empires and larger governing bodies, and the appointment of rulers without competitive elections. Actors within states experiencing the transition from Communist rule have been some of the latest to use the referendum device for a variety of purposes.

The politics of referendums, or, more accurately, the *strategies* used to call and hold referendums have been the same in different types of political systems across the globe and throughout history. Referendums are prone to manipulation through the wording used for the question, the timing of the vote, its subject matter, whether or not it is actually held, and the interpretation of the results from votes that have taken place. Referendum campaigns can take advantage of the fact that the popular will is not often perfectly translated through the use of these votes and can often be crafted by actors. Specifically, referendum campaigns make plain the different goals between the elites and masses within a society, and the bargaining that takes place between elites. The essential concept at the center of this elite bargaining is nothing other than *power*: who has it and who can gain more of it usually at another's expense. Specifically, it is the distribution of power among actors between and within their respective institutional settings that is the key to this story. This elite bargaining over power often takes place in the competition between executives and legislatures. Executives often attempt to force legislatures to adopt policies it would not otherwise accept if not for the popular legitimacy of a referendum.

The actor who is left out of this "two-person, zero-sum" game is the people. When executives and legislators are attempting to maximize their power in order to implement policies they believe are right, the people are only important with respect to elite calculations about how they would vote in a referendum. This is almost always the case with referendums that are not constitutionally mandated; votes that must be taken on certain issues demanded by a constitution have much less strategic calculation involved though they may be just as political. Achieving a simple majority of those citizens voting in a contest is not only an art but also has become a science. The use of the media, especially in a well-funded campaign, has been shown in several instances to be unfair (Broder 2000). Because equality is an essential component of democracy (Dahl 1998), this study argues that the kind of manipulation possible in referendum campaigns strains the very democratic nature of the process itself.

Therefore this book is not just about referendums but also about the distribution of power, the role of legitimacy, and the nature of democracy. These key concepts, along with bargaining and strategy, cannot be divorced from this discussion. Referendums are not inherently democratic just because they measure the will of the people through popular votes. Legitimacy can be bestowed in principled and unprincipled ways. Elites attempt to fulfill their separate goals in a bargaining process that is more defined by power than not. Referendums are simply the latest and most fascinating way that these kinds of politics have been playing out.

This study makes the following arguments in order to show that referendum politics utilize the same, basic mechanism. This mechanism may play out differently in different environments and times, and may even evolve to solve a variety of problems; nevertheless, the basic mechanism is the same:

(1) Referendums are part of a bargaining process between elites who have their basis of power in different institutional settings.
(2) Referendums give political actors the political legitimacy to pursue change and potentially alter status quo institutions.
(3) Executives can better position themselves than legislatures along a policy spectrum to win when introducing referendums.

Evidence for the first two arguments will be gathered and presented in referendum case studies from France, Chile, the Soviet Union, and Russia in chapters 2, 3, and 4. The third argument suggests several hypotheses that may be tested with the Large-N Data Set on Post-Soviet states in chapter 5:

(3.1) If executives can better position themselves along a policy spectrum, they should propose a greater number of referendums than legislatures.
(3.2) If executives can better position themselves along a policy spectrum, they should win a greater number of referendums than legislatures.

A General Theory of Referendum Politics

The arguments about the use of referendums by executives and other actors is theoretically based in rational choice theory and is tested by the entire set of proposed referendums in the Soviet and Post-Soviet states from 1990–1997. The spatial models used in this work do not form the single, theoretical basis for the arguments being made; rather, they illustrate part of the elite calculations that are postulated to take place. *The theoretical heart of this work is a rational, bargaining framework that takes place between elites in different institutional settings who have the option of using the referendum device to resolve disputes.* Elites are viewed as making rational calculations concerning their interests and those of the people they represent; elites express these interests through their preferences. Elites attempt to fulfill these preferences in order to maximize their payoffs; in other words, to reap whatever material and/or psychological rewards they perceive as being able to fulfill.

In game theoretic terms, a referendum is essentially a two-person, zero-sum game. The elite actors are usually political executives and legislatures in competition with one another; however, referendums can be fought between any number of actors or coalitions of actors within a state. As the main proponents and opponents of a referendum decide which moves to make relative to the other, the people decide the outcome of the referendum vote. However, the people do not play a central role in the bargaining process; nature, or chance, would represent their vote in a referendum game.

Though this work focuses upon political elites in institutional positions of power in France, Chile, and the Post-Soviet states, the observations made can be generalized beyond this set of countries and their respective time periods. In order to fulfill their preferences, or strategic goals, political elites will attempt to garner more power for themselves and their institutions. In other words, elites as goal-seekers are often attempting to maximize their power in order to gain influence over political debates. This bargaining does not go easily not only because they are in competition with one another but also because they and their institutions are often characterized by a lack of power—this is especially true during transitions. Power is normally derived from sources of legitimacy and authority, but during transitions, especially from Communism, old sources of legitimacy and authority have been discredited. Therefore they have turned to the people—the most valid source of political legitimacy in our time.[3] This process extends to institutions in stable democracies because quite often these institutions are plagued by weaknesses themselves, some of which may be constitutionally derived in a system of checks and balances.

The people grant political legitimacy through electoral institutions; these institutions, however, come in at least two different forms—those of direct democracy, like referendums, and those of representative democracy, like regular elections for legislators. Though some have argued that the distinction between direct and representative democracy is a false one (Mendelsohn and Parkin 2001, 1), this work sees an important distinction and recognizes the real tension between legislators and direct democracy. Elites, in an attempt to confer legitimacy on themselves, their policies, and their institutions, have learned by the example of history and practice that the referendum device can confer not only legitimacy but also establish a new distribution of power between institutions and the elites who make them up.

But what makes elites seek to change the status quo between institutions? During transitions and in some stable polities institutions are not only weak but also relatively equal because of their weakness. Some might argue that this equal "balance of power" between institutions might serve to placate any desires by elites to change the status quo especially if that change is not guaranteed to benefit their respective institutions. The game theoretic literature on international relations dealing with bargaining and power suggests that an even distribution of power between two states is not a stable situation if the use of force may result in a situation different from the status quo (Powell 1996b). This describes a very similar situation to an even distribution of power not only between states but also between institutions like an executive and a legislature.[4] Proposing and/or calling a referendum can be seen similarly in a bargaining context to the use of force.

Elites will use referendums to garner legitimacy and therefore win a policy debate if they believe that the people favor their position over their opponent. During transitions and certain openings in stable polities, elites will take the use of referendums one step further by seeking to change the distribution of power between their respective institutions if they believe the people support the strengthening of their institution to the detriment of their opponents' institutions. The logic of this calculation is similar once again to the logic of state behavior with respect to a distribution of benefits correlating to an underlying distribution of power (Powell 1999, 85). In terms of this study, therefore, if both the executive and legislature are weak and have comparable power, then one would seek to call a referendum if one can expect to win and have the policy dispute decided in one's favor.

The Use of Spatial Models

If an executive understands its position and that of the legislature and the people on an issue in a political debate, the executive will be enticed to call a referendum to garner an electoral victory because of advantages he or she may possess. First, however, this study must introduce and discuss a method by which we can analyze elite and mass positions in a policy debate. The politics of referendums can be illustrated with the use of spatial models that show the relative positions of the electorate and political elites in a policy space (see figure 1.1). In these models we will assume that the actors have single-peaked preferences: this means that an actor's opinion on a subject is clear and undivided and can be expressed as a point on a policy space. The preferences of actors made up of many individuals, such as a legislature or the "people," may still be single-peaked even though they can be expressed as a range of opinion on a

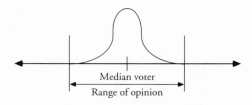

Median voter

Range of opinion

Figure 1.1   The range of opinion and the median voter

policy space—this is known as the ideal point of the median voter (Morrow 1994, 104–5).[5]

When a range of opinion is shown, as in figure 1.1, it should be inferred that a single-peaked preference lies approximately in its middle. This middle is usually expressed as the median voter with regard to the electorate; the median voter represents the theoretical median of opinion held by an electorate, legislature, or similar voting body. The vertical axis, not highlighted in the one-dimensional models in this work but implicit in figure 1.1, is a measure of popular votes from the electorate and is expressed by the graph of a "hump."

Spatial models usually only deal with a policy space in one dimension. This is a significant simplification given the fact that many policy debates include discussions along several dimensions, for example marketization and political liberalization often go hand-in-hand not only in the Post-Soviet cases but also throughout the rest of the world that is transitioning to democracy. Nevertheless, a very strong argument can be made for the use of a one-dimensional policy space: referendum questions, correctly or incorrectly, actually simplify policy debates into one dimension. Referendums ask a yes or no, up or down question usually on one issue even if a more complicated policy debate is implied. It is the very essence of a referendum to simplify—some would argue oversimplify—a policy debate. For example, even though a question might explicitly ask for the public's view on marketization there is often an underlying question regarding political liberalization. Nevertheless, this attribute of the referendum will allow this simplification if we proceed carefully and do not fail to discuss the complexity of each policy debate.

Sometimes referendums ask more than one question at a time similar to the April 1993 Russian referendums that addressed: (1) trust in Boris Yeltsin, (2) approval of Yeltsin's socioeconomic policies, (3) early elections for the Russian presidency, and (4) early elections for the Congress of People's Deputies. Technically, when a referendum includes more than one question, each question is considered a "referendum" for the sake of this study. Therefore, the April 1993 Russian vote was actually four referendums held at the same time on different questions.

"Carryover" Institutions

Carryover institutions are defined as those whose members, leaders, and/or preferences reflect a prior status quo based upon a set of rules or a political environment distinctly different from the present. This prior status quo, especially during transitions, is often out of step, even if just slightly, with the median voter. It is in this way that an executive may have an advantage positioning itself with voters with respect to a legislature that is a holdover from a Communist regime, for example. Figure 1.2 illustrates three cases in which an executive (E) can take advantage of a legislature's position (L) in a policy space that goes from the most liberal/non-Communist politics to the most non-liberal/ Communist political position.[6] In the Post-Soviet, Russian experience, the legislature is often out of step with the people (P) in that they have usually been more Communist and less liberal than, for example, a majority of the Russian people.

Case 1 illustrates an example of where the legislature (L) as a whole is more Communist and less liberal than a majority of the Russian people (P); this situation could occur as a result of a legislature that has been a holdover from the Communist era. The people never wholly elected such legislatures; all or part of the legislative body was appointed and/or drawn from Communist organizations. These are prime examples of *carryover* institutions, and they play an extremely important role in Post-Soviet politics. This is one of the reasons why executives (E) have a better opportunity to be closer to the people (P) on any particular issue; in the diagram, both the people (P) and the executive (E) are to the left of the legislature (L).

Case 2 illustrates the example where a legislature's leadership (Lx) is a holdover from the Communist regime. In this situation, the executive wants to initiate a policy but the leadership in the legislature does not want to consider it. In this case the legislature as a whole might favor the idea but the leadership will not even put it on the agenda. Once again, in this diagram, the people (P) and the executive (E) are to the left of the legislature's leadership.

Case 3 illustrates an example where the true preferences of the legislature (Lt) lay within a majority view of the people (P) but the

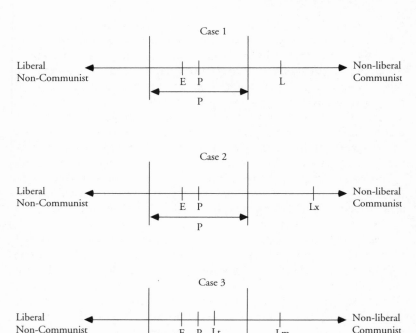

Key:
E, Executive
L, Legislature
Lx, Leg.'s leadership
Lt, Leg.'s true preference
Lm, Leg.'s manifest preference
|←P→|, The "People's" preferences

Figure 1.2 Spatial modeling of referendum actors: three cases

legislature's manifest preferences (Lm) put it outside of the people's view. A legislature's manifest preferences are a skewed version of its true preferences that allow it to avoid the public consequences of its true position on an issue. Though the legislature and executive (E) may agree on an issue, the legislature may not want to reveal its true preferences because of a fear of electoral consequences. This unique situation may be the result of how the legislature is districted, especially if it was redistricted during its members' tenures. If the legislature is a *carryover* institution, it may be risk-averse to alerting the people that it no longer represents them well.

Categorizing Referendums: Autonomy, Constitutional, and Policy Votes

Though all referendum votes are arguably important, not all referendums are of equal concern to domestic political elites and the electorate. Political actors and the people often place differing amounts of importance on referendums based upon their effects. A referendum calling for independence of a state sub-unit from a federal structure will cause a great deal of political debate and strife to most. However, a referendum that proposes a change in a legislature from a unicameral to a bicameral institution raises stakes the most among political elites in the unicameral body. Therefore progress in understanding referendums requires the categorization of different types of referendums. This categorization, though used throughout this book, will have greater significance in chapter 5 when we attempt to discern if executives have an advantage with respect to referendums.

After reviewing the literature, I have organized these votes into three categories by their subject matter.[7] These categories progress from dealing with relations between states (*autonomy*) to relations concerning the Constitution of a state (*constitutional*) to the policies that directly affect the citizenry of a state (*policy*). Autonomy referendums are votes that deal with a state's independence from or integration into a larger governmental body. Examples include votes for independence from an empire or state and integration into international organizations such as the European Union or NATO. Constitutional referendums are votes that deal with how a state's government should be structured and which institutions hold what power. Examples include votes called to ratify constitutions, set executive/legislative powers, and decide between presidential and parliamentary government. Policy referendums are votes that deal with internal matters directly affecting a state's mass population as a whole. These votes may also highlight and antagonize differences between majority and minority groups within a state. Examples include those votes that set economic policy, set state language, change official names of cities or other public entities, and approve private land ownership.

Another categorization that seems to make sense would be by who initiates the vote: an executive seeking a vote of confidence, an individual or group using a referendum as a populist instrument, or just a group of citizens seeking to have their voice heard could form another categorization. However, in practice, this categorization is not quite obvious and tends to provide more confusion than clarity. Another type of referendum that might need to be categorized is constitutionally mandated referendums that by law must be called in certain situations; these votes can also be manipulated by elites for political gain. In general, because it is not always clear *who* is calling a referendum vote and *why*, this study has simply focused upon a categorization based upon subject matter.

Referendums Provide Political Legitimacy in the Modern World

Nor should we listen to those who say, "The voice of the people is the voice of God," for the turbulence of the mob is always close to insanity.

Alcuin (Flaccus Albinus Alcuinus) of York
(753–804) English scholar

Modern democracies draw their authority not from kings or divine sanction but from the will of the people and the states of the former Soviet Union have proven to be no exception.[8] Old sources of authority and legitimacy have been discredited with the decline of the Communist Party and the Communist ideology. Therefore it has been important for politicians to legitimize their policy proposals through devices that confer legitimacy by professedly measuring the will of the public (Bendix 1978). By claiming to measure the will of the people, electoral institutions in general and referendums in particular have become the voice of the people.

In the transition from Communism, the former republics of the Soviet Union have utilized popular elections and referendums in order to choose their political leaders and their policies. Moreover, the referendum device has been used to legitimate new constitutions, pass treaties, and grant personal legitimacy to politicians and their policies. In fact, politicians have utilized referendums to legitimate remaining in office for a subsequent term without elections and implementing controversial policies against the objection of their opponents. To this and other ends the referendum device was proposed and/or used 152 times between 1990 and 1997 throughout the Soviet and Post-Soviet states. In sum, referendums play an increasingly important role in transitions because they have the ability to grant political legitimacy and power by conferring the mandate of the people. Reinhard Bendix (1978) said it best: "In our time, not only democracies but also military regimes, dictatorships, and even constitutional monarchies are legitimized by claims of popular mandate. Indeed, other ways of justifying authority have become inconceivable."

The voice of the people, or the popular mandate, in turn, was once referred to as the voice of God. The people's will was thought to be so legitimate that it was equated with divine authority; in essence the people's will was given divine sanction. However, another title for this work could be *Vox Caesaris Vox Populi*, which is derived from the old Latin phrase, "Vox populi vox Dei," or in English, "the voice of the people is the voice of God." Alcuin of York quoted these words in a letter to Charlemagne not as an endorsement but as a warning that popular sentiment is erratic and carries anything but the stamp of divine authority. Correspondingly, social science has shown that the electorate may never clearly express the people's will when it votes (Arrow 1950; Ordeshook 1986, 57–9). Moreover, because the wording of a referendum question, the timing of a referendum vote, and its interpretation afterwards can all be manipulated by elites, the ends to which referendum votes are applied is not above question. Leaders who occasionally put their own self-interest above that of their constituents or simply conflate the two may find even greater incentive to do so during transition times if the very institution—like an executive or legislature—they belong to is threatened by change. Given the vulnerability of the people's will to manipulation and misinterpretation by political leaders, the phrase "Vox populi vox Dei" might be updated to "Vox Caesaris vox populi" or "The voice of Caesar is the voice of the people." Nowhere was this aphorism more relevant than in the Post-Soviet transition.

Referendums Play a Crucial Role in Bargaining Between Political Elites

The study of referendums in the Soviet and Post-Soviet states from 1990 to 1997 highlights the elite bargaining that took place in their transitions from Communism. These referendums could hardly have called themselves, written themselves, and done their own lobbying. Political leaders did so to further their goal of staying in power; this goal, especially during transitions, may diverge from what the people want. Moreover there is sometimes no regularized way—such as elections—for the people to express effectively their preferences during transitions. Given the power of these devices to grant legitimacy to policies and individuals after the fall of Communism, referendum votes captured the attention of both public officials and private citizens. Referendum votes on various topics became hard-fought battles between reformers and conservatives, executives and legislatures, and federal government structures and regions.

Referendums can determine the outcome of a policy or political debate by granting legitimacy to a position or politician. Executive actors—presidents, prime ministers, and general secretaries—often face off against legislative opponents—congresses, parliaments, soviets, councils, and standing committees—in competitions in an attempt to fulfill their political goals. Referendums introduce a third actor—the people—that can have the significant effect of tipping the balance of power toward one actor or another.

Referendums in the Fifth Republic of France and in Chile in the 1970s and 1980s, discussed in chapter 2, show how executives use referendums in elite bargaining and preview their usage in the Post-Soviet states. Former president Charles de Gaulle of France and former president Augusto Pinochet of Chile used the referendum device to grant legitimacy to themselves, their policies, and their institutional bases of power. Their struggles pitted the executive against the legislature, or some would say the dictator against the masses. Nevertheless, what made their use of the referendum device exceptional is the degree to which a "personal" connection with the people through the legitimizing voice of the referendum was prized. These case studies demonstrate the validity of the first two arguments of this manuscript: referendums should be viewed as part of the bargaining process and referendums can legitimate change and alter status quo institutions.

Referendums in the Soviet Union in 1991, discussed in chapter 3, show other facets of elite bargaining when the referendum device is introduced. Mikhail Gorbachev, the former general secretary of the Communist Party and president of the Soviet Union, specifically introduced the referendum device into the Soviet and Post-Soviet context in order to use the legitimacy of the people to outflank his political opponents. Gorbachev attempted to head off the dissolution of the Soviet Union into its constituent republics by holding a union-wide vote on maintaining the federal structure. This spawned a plethora of autonomy counter-referendums by republics seeking some degree of independence or at the very least wishing to establish a legitimacy to govern outside of Soviet Communism. These cases demonstrate how the referendum device was introduced into the region and how elites bargain and change the distribution of power not only between executives and legislatures but also between institutions of different federal and regional structures.

Referendums in Russia in 1993, discussed in chapter 4, show the role these devices play in bargaining and conflict between an executive and a legislature in the Post-Soviet states. Boris Yeltsin, former president of Russia, began with a huge advantage after the break-up of the Soviet Union as the first popularly elected president of Russia. Nevertheless, he still encountered stiff opposition from the Congress of People's Deputies and its chairman Ruslan Khasbulatov. In fact, Ruslan Khasbulatov attempted to turn the referendums around on Yeltsin in an effort not only to challenge the popularity of Yeltsin's programs but also to call for new presidential elections. In the end, these referendums show both how they can fail to resolve conflict over policy in April 1993 and how they can legitimize a strong presidential system in December 1993 with a vote on a new Russian constitution.

Referendums Change the Distribution of Power Between Institutions

Referendums can be used in substantially different situations and thus have different effects, for example, depending on whether they are used in times of stability or transition. In times of stability, referendums usually grant legitimacy to policy positions and sometimes to individual politicians but almost never change the distribution of power between institutions. Referendums shift the balance of power in a political debate by introducing the will of the people.

In transition periods, however, referendums can change the distribution of power between institutions.[9] Elites understand that when referendums confer legitimacy to individuals and policies, they can also confer legitimacy to political institutions and change the distribution of power between institutions in fluid times. Strong institutions, like the executive in the beginning of the Fifth Republic of France, continue to strengthen when leaders like Charles de Gaulle deftly use the referendum device to change the distribution of power in favor of themselves and the executive. As a matter of definition, strong institutions can effectively both define and implement policies within a state. Weak institutions have trouble effectively defining and implementing policies, and may have less influence than other institutions, interest groups, and other societal actors.[10]

In the latter part of 1990 and in 1991, Soviet institutions were weak because of the challenges to Communism symbolized by the dissolution of the East European Bloc and Mikhail Gorbachev's programs of *glasnost* and *perestroika* (McFaul 1995; Van Atta 1989). Gorbachev used the referendum device in March 1991 with the hope of garnering legitimacy for a new union treaty to hold the state together; the referendum, however, also spawned counter-referendums from republics seeking independence or greater autonomy. Many Soviet republics used the referendum device to legitimate their secession movements; a few of them even held their independence votes before Gorbachev held the USSR-wide referendum on the union.[11]

Though few institutions during transition periods may be considered strong, some institutions hold advantages over others. Early in the transition from Communism, institutions and elites in the Post-Soviet sphere were weak as one might imagine (McFaul 1995; Walker 1993). But legislatures, compared to executives, were at a distinct disadvantage because they were *carryover* institutions and out of step with the people. *Carryover* institutions, as noted earlier, are defined as those whose members, leaders, and/or preferences reflect a prior status quo based upon a set of rules or a political environment distinctly different from the present. The Russian Congress of People's Deputies from 1992 to 1993 is a perfect example of a *carryover* institution. This Congress was originally elected in Russia in 1990 under Gorbachev's tenure and while its members were elected in multi-candidate races, these elections were not multiparty. Well into 1993, most of its members still represented the ideas of the old Communist Party as well as, for example, large state enterprises and collectivized agriculture.

Even though executives in the Post-Soviet states were also weak, they were more successful in finding mechanisms not only to implement reform policies that were inevitably controversial in a state experiencing both marketization and democratization but also to strengthen their own institutions. Executives and other groups soon learned that the referendum device was one such mechanism. Boris Yeltsin, for example, used the referendum device to remake Russia into a presidential republic with a strong presidency and a weak parliament in December 1993.

In times of transition, therefore, the important distinction between referendums is whether they simply seek policy change or a change in the distribution of power between institutions. Referendums that change the distribution of power between the executive and legislature, or the federal center and the regions, can have effects that last for generations. In the short term, the ability to change the distribution of power between institutions raises the stakes between referendum proponents and opponents.

Moreover, calling a referendum may raise the stakes between political opponents and exacerbate an already tense situation; in other words, referendums may serve as an intermediate, or proximate, cause of conflict hibernating beneath the surface. The Russian April 1993 referendums are a good example of how referendum politics can not only fail to resolve political stalemate but also possibly lead to violence. The relationship between referendums and conflict will be explored in several places in this book. It will be shown that referendums can reveal conflict within a polity and can either resolve, exacerbate, or have little effect upon a tense situation.

Ethnic groups also used referendums to grant legitimacy to their cause; a common occurrence is when majorities use a referendum to legitimize policies unwanted by minorities (Butler and Ranney 1978, 36). In the Post-Soviet states, the politics surrounding *autonomy* and *policy* referendums often include a Russian majority subjecting others to a popular vote for an unwanted expression of opinion—a nonbinding vote—or legitimization of law. Leaders of the Soviet Union and Russia have also used the existence of Russian minority populations within former Soviet states as a reason for reintegration of the empire or as an excuse to interfere with their domestic affairs.

Specifically, the inclusion of ethnicity as a factor is closely related to the politics of *autonomy* referendums and the continuing *fission* of the Post-Soviet states: the tendency of subareas, units, or regions of a state seeking independence that continue to breakdown into smaller and smaller regions. The break-up of the Soviet Union is the prime example of this process; republics, who have now become states, are now facing autonomy challenges from their own constituent parts—Chechnya in Russia being the most well-known example. Referendums have contributed to this phenomenon by giving regions a tool to legitimize their desires and claims of independence. Though the impetus of this process stems from a combination of inter-ethnic dynamics and pure elite ambition, it would be harder for the leaders of these regions to demand their independence without the polls that demonstrate that the people are in favor of sovereignty.

In transition periods, the role of the executive and its use of the referendum device can either help lead a country toward a strong democracy or toward a weak democracy or authoritarian state. Executives interested in democratic reform may have to face *carryover* institutions in the form of legislatures, independence-minded subregions, and illiberal forces (e.g., the military or the Communist Party). Sometimes executives must attempt to balance instituting reforms that have the goal of democratization against maintaining continuity of culture or provoking unrest—though these goals are not necessarily mutually exclusive they are certainly hard to accomplish at the same time in transition politics. Executives interested in autocracy may use the referendum device to strengthen their position nominally so that they can "save" democracy but in reality so that their power, and authority, has been consolidated. Another question, therefore, concerning referendums is whether their use leads to democracy and stability or to something else.

Other Explanations of Referendum and Legislative Behavior

This book, though focusing upon the executive use of the referendum, aims to fill a gap in the scholarly literature with a cross-national, comparative perspective on the use of referendums—one of the first such works along with Mads Qvortrup's *A Comparative Study of Referendums: Government by the People* (2002). David Butler and Austin Ranney in 1978 edited the first comprehensive, theoretical work on referendums in general. Their second installment *Referendums Around the World* (1994) contained the first analysis of referendums in the former Soviet Union and Eastern Europe by Henry Brady and Cynthia Kaplan. Brady and Kaplan's chapter focuses on empirical data and suggests many good theoretical questions. A working paper by Ronald J. Hill and Stephen White (1995) provides a more descriptive account of referendums in Russia while a chapter in a later book does much of the same (White et al. 1997). Several edited volumes on referendums in Europe (Gallagher and Uleri 1996) and even in Eastern and Central Europe (Auer and Bützer 2001) have added to our collective knowledge.

Some of the prior theoretical work has explained a state legislature's response to an initiative[12] (Gerber 1996a), the effect of money and interest groups on referendums (Gerber 1999), and the logic of initiative action in California (Cain and Spiller 1991). Some of the work on direct democracy has analyzed referendums through the lens of democratic theory (Cronin 1989; Setälä 1999) along with some recent theories from the social sciences (Haskell 2001). *The Strategic Use of Referendums* aims to contribute both theoretically and empirically to the scholarly literature on referendums—a literature that is small but growing in size and importance—by observing continuities in their use.

This study recognizes two alternative models of legislative behavior that are instructive with respect to referendum politics: the delegate model and the institutional model (Gerber 1996b). In the delegate model, the views of constituents determine the behavior of legislators which is similar to spatial voting models of reelection-oriented legislators (Mayhew 1974; Downs 1957). Thus over a single dimension these delegates usually choose the policy positions of the median voter in their districts. In this way, because the legislature is a collection of representatives who themselves do not stray far from the median voter of their districts, the legislature as a whole reflects a "median of medians," which may restrict it from flexibly relocating its position (Gerber 1996b). Moreover, what if the legislature has been constructed to represent interests other than those of voters in districts? The Russian Congress of People's Deputies from 1992 to 1993, as noted earlier, included members who still represented, for example, large state enterprises and collectivized agriculture, which could have put it at odds with the median Russian voter. Therefore, the executive may be more likely to call a referendum because it has a greater flexibility in locating itself near the median voter than the more intransigent, and out of step, legislature.

In the institutional model, legislative behavior can also be understood as a response to incentives and constraints introduced by the legislative institution (Gerber 1996b). This model suggests the importance of factors other than voters such as party and party leadership (Cox and McCubbins 1993; Erikson et al. 1993; Rohde 1991; Sinclair 1983; Cooper and Brady 1981), legislative committees (Kiewiet and McCubbins 1991; Collie and Cooper 1989; Hall 1989), and the influence of contributions (Romer and Snyder 1994). Therefore legislators in the institutional model have multiple goals, which may include power and position within the legislature, policy outcomes, and legislative coalitions (Gerber 1996b; Fenno 1973). Party, parliamentary leaders, and legislative coalitions have had a significant impact on legislative behavior in the Soviet and Post-Soviet cases with respect to referendum politics because the position of a legislature often depended more upon the particular results of elite bargaining rather than a simple calculation of voter interests or needs. Therefore legislative behavior toward referendums has often been dictated by concerns other than the position of the median voter, and therefore, has allowed openings for the executive to exploit divergences of position between the voters and the legislature on an issue.

Uncertainties about Referendums with Respect to Legitimacy and Democracy

Direct popular votes seem to be simple devices of direct democracy, but referendums often challenge our notions of legitimacy. There are a host of questions that need answers, for example: Why do referendums fail to resolve issues they were called to address? How does one define exactly a successful referendum result? Successful referendums confer a legitimacy that is recognized not only by those sponsoring a referendum but also by those opposed to it. Why are referendum questions often ambiguous? Leaders often use ambiguous questions to allow them to manipulate the results to their goals, but when referendums yield unclear results, a vote may not have the desired effect because other political actors may decide to interpret the vote in their own way. Votes may be complicated by differences in national versus regional vote tallies: for example, certain regions within a state may reject a vote while it passes overall—does it matter? Votes may also fall along regional lines and be coupled with issues of group identity, ethnicity, and substate secession that raise the stakes for those involved. The simplicity of the referendum device gives way quickly to contentious political debates.

The fact that referendums have now become a part of state transitions to democracy when their usage has not been well understood in consolidated democracies is not only ironic but also unfortunate. The demand for popularly legitimated regimes will only increase as more and more traditional sources of authority wither away. This work will attempt to answer these and many more questions in the upcoming chapters. The study of how leaders have begun to use referendums to supply regimes with legitimacy correctly begins with the study of the Fifth Republic of France and Charles de Gaulle. De Gaulle's spirited use of the referendum device not only served as a model for other state leaders in the twentieth century but also demonstrates how executives attempt to use this device to connect *personally* with the people.

CHAPTER 2

Referendums and Executives in France and Chile

R eferendums were a central part of the bargaining process between political elites in France's Fifth Republic and at the very least a device that was meant to legitimate the actions of elites in Chile in the 1970s and 1980s. Both Charles de Gaulle and Augusto Pinochet were elites in executive positions of power who had risen through the ranks of the military. Both de Gaulle and Pinochet looked down upon the messiness of representative democracy with, from their perspective, its squabbling parties, indecisiveness, and perceived weakness to make and set correct policy. Both viewed the referendum device as a way not only to legitimate what they viewed as better policies but also to change the distribution of power between political institutions. The cases detailed in this chapter provide a vivid, compelling preview of how executives would often use the referendum device during transitions to democracy in the Post-Soviet states. In particular, these cases show how executives use the referendum to make "personal" connections with the people—a connection they always see as an important legitimizing factor in their bargaining with other political elites.

The usual result of executive–legislative political conflict within the Post-Soviet states has been the establishment of strong executives. Leaders have argued that strong executives, mostly in the form of strong presidents, are needed in order to see the transition from Communism to democracy through. Most executives—including Boris Yeltsin, Ukrainian Presidents Kravchuk and Kuchma, and Askar Akayev of Kyrgyzstan— have argued for presidential systems rather than parliamentary systems. They have argued that antidemocratic and antiprogressive interests dominate the legislatures, or parliaments, and have therefore worked toward increasing the power of the president while decreasing the power of parliament. This trend toward strong executives has renewed the debate on the merits of presidential versus parliamentary systems in Western academic circles.

Executives in the Post-Soviet states have made an indirect argument against investing in the establishment of political parties by citing the perceived lack of utility of parties in the direct election of an executive—that is, a president, governor, or mayor. Political parties tend to flourish, they argue, in the day-to-day workings and multiple local election campaigns of legislatures more than in the single election campaign for a statewide president. Though parties have become important in electing a president in the United States and other established democracies, presidential elections have not yet helped in the establishment of parties in the Post-Soviet states. Therefore instead of promoting the development of political parties, executives have utilized the referendum device to legitimize the establishment of presidential systems.

The modern prototypical example of this use of the referendum device has been by Charles de Gaulle in his establishment of the Fifth Republic in France. De Gaulle's dislike for political parties and the French Parliament is well documented (Frears 1977; Berstein 1993, 8–11; Lacouture 1991, 203–4). He believed that they formed an impediment to his goal of making France unified and strong. Constitutionally, de Gaulle could not propose a referendum; all referendums needed to be proposed by both houses of the French Parliament or the government (Constitution of the French Fifth Republic, article 11). Therefore, de Gaulle would have his prime minister make referendum proposals to Parliament with the caveat that he would resign if they did not call his referendum (Frears 1977; Lacouture 1991; Hayward 1969). Because he believed himself to be essential to the establishment of the French republic, he bet throughout his career in public office that Parliament would not deny him. Likewise, de Gaulle always presented the referendum vote to the people as a choice between his suggested and well-publicized voting preference and his resignation. De Gaulle made a practice of conflating his personal legitimacy with that of the state, and it was never more explicit than in his use of the referendum device.

By threatening to resign, de Gaulle illustrates another way in which an actor can manipulate a referendum vote. The people's preferences on how to vote are affected by their expectation of how things might change if they do or do not support de Gaulle's position on the referendum issue. It is a choice between voting for de Gaulle's position and the results that would follow or not supporting de Gaulle's position and the *reversion point* (Romer and Rosenthal 1979). This *reversion point* could either be a continuation of the status quo if de Gaulle does not resign or a worse outcome if de Gaulle's threat to resign is realized. De Gaulle therefore manipulates the *reversion point* in an attempt to force the voters to accept his referendum position.

From his opponents' perspective, de Gaulle's use of the referendum device was part of his personal agenda to delegitimize and decrease the power of Parliament. For his opponents, de Gaulle's use of the referendum was not simply to gauge the people's will upon an issue but was also aimed at subverting the power of the legislature. To them, de Gaulle's policy goals did not require the disenfranchisement of the legislature. Pierre Mendés-France, a prominent leader of the Left, said in 1968: "Plebiscites? You don't discuss them, you fight them."[1] From de Gaulle's perspective, decreasing the power of Parliament went a long way in helping to establish the French republic he desired. Charles de Gaulle's use of the referendum often enhanced his own legitimacy and/or institutional power whether or not his positions represented the interests of the citizenry. De Gaulle used referendums to legitimate his policy choices by making each vote a vote of confidence in him; de Gaulle, for example, explicitly made clear that any vote against one of his referendums was a vote against himself. He lived up to Louis XIV's saying, "L'état c'est moi."[2]

In the end, though, the conflation of personal legitimacy with that of the referendum vote led to de Gaulle's resignation from office.[3] De Gaulle's last and unsuccessful use of the referendum device was an attempt to devolve power away from his opponents in the Senate, one of the two chambers of Parliament, by giving more power to local municipalities. Earlier, de Gaulle had used a referendum to give the office of the president, his office, the ability to be directly elected by the people instead of being elected through Parliament.

Similarly, Augusto Pinochet's use of the referendum device in Chile also led to his downfall. While de Gaulle's opposition came in the form of elites concentrated in the French Senate, Pinochet's opposition consisted of a fragmented majority of Chilean society and resembled a poor people's movement. Pinochet's opposition successfully organized itself against the vote on a grass roots level in a way that rejuvenated the electorate. In the 1980 Constitution Pinochet helped design, the military rulers of Chile had promised in eight years to hold a referendum on whether the regime should continue or if elections should be held. In this way Pinochet's authority was directly linked to the popular mandate. Nevertheless, he could have postponed the vote. Instead, he decided to

hold it believing strongly that the people he had oppressed and sometimes killed over the past 15 years would not only forgive him but also
praise him for the modicum of economic success the country had expe-
rienced in the 1980s. Instead, the people voted to hold elections that
essentially ended Pinochet's tenure as head of state and began a period
of transition from authoritarian rule to democracy.[4]

Even though their advisors constantly warned them of the possibility,
both de Gaulle and Pinochet persevered in holding referendum votes
that opinion polls had determined they would lose. Entwined in their
own cults of personality, both executives may have believed their popularity among their constituents would insure victory. Even though
de Gaulle enjoyed substantial support among the electorate in the 1960s
(Berstein 1993, ch. 8), French voters were solidly against devolving
power away from the Senate (Hayward 1969, 294–5; Lacouture 1991,
571–4). The basis of Pinochet's optimism is even harder to explain
though it has been suggested that he always believed the military would
not allow another candidate to take office (Villagran 1988, 4).[5]
Irrespective of specific motivations, they seemed wholly to ignore the
information given to them through polling.

An analysis of these French and Chilean cases will yield a general
model of referendum politics that can be used in the analysis of other
referendum cases. In this way a *modal*, or typical, model of referendum
politics can be established before we analyze the somewhat more complicated Soviet and Post-Soviet referendums. Though the specific details of
political situations may differ, leaders often find the goals, incentives,
and institutional devices in their control to be the same.

Referendums in the French Fifth Republic

Referendums have a long and somewhat sullied history in France. Under
Napoleon Bonaparte's instruction, France held a constitutional referendum in 1799 on the use of the referendum device that has been
described as a "*de facto* plebiscite."[6] It was both the first referendum held
in France and the first held in any country statewide in modern times.
In 1802, Napoleon used the referendum to ask the public "shall he be
consul for life."[7] In 1852, Louis Napoleon used the referendum to legitimize his coup d'état and "declared that he had only infringed legality to
return to the fundamental law, *vox populi*."[8] These votes gave referendums a deservedly bad reputation. Hence, whenever a leader has used
a referendum to prolong his stay in office in the absence of an election
or to justify a coup d'état, many scholars will refer to it as *Bonapartist*

(Frears 1977, 239). Likewise, Hitler's use of this device in the 1930s to legitimize his regime gave the word *plebiscite* in the twentieth century a bad name (Butler and Ranney 1978, 3–4).[9] However, referendums and plebiscites describe the exact same function.

In France, the referendum was used three times during the Fourth Republic—once in 1945 and twice in 1946—in order to confirm its constitution. The successful 1945 vote only asked if the citizenry wanted a new constitution while the May 1946 vote to adopt the new constitution failed. Because the constitution of the Fourth Republic was finally ratified by referendum in October 1946 with a significantly smaller portion of the electorate than the failed vote of May 1946—the turnout in October was 68.8 percent of the electorate compared to 80.7 percent in May—many felt the legitimacy of the regime was compromised (Bertier de Sauvigny and Pinkney 1983, 369; Butler and Ranney 1978, 229). As it turns out, the Fourth Republic lasted little more than ten years from 1947 to 1958.

The Fourth Republic was plagued with an instability and ineffectiveness that manifested itself in government coalitions often made up of three or more parties that could not remain united. Almost every issue divided the ruling coalition and made governing ineffective. The parliamentary system set up under the 1946 Constitution included the office of president, but it was a figurehead position. Most of the power lay with the National Assembly. The second chamber, named the Council of the Republic, was weak relative to the National Assembly. Though technically an absolute majority was required by the National Assembly to appoint and depose a prime minister, various procedures were instituted that effectively made the rule void (Bertier de Sauvigny and Pinkney 1983, 369). This led to chronic ministerial instability and 24 different governments coming and going between December 1946 and May 1958. Nevertheless, the Fourth Republic's collapse was triggered by the Algerian crisis. Like most colonies in Africa after World War II, Algeria was moving toward independence. The French European generals and their forces resisted this move with increasing violence and threats not only against the Algerians but also against the French government for their lack of support. The crisis became so serious that Parisians began to expect French Algerian-based paratroopers to begin landing in the streets. In May 1958, the Algerian generals formed the Committee of Public Safety and took power. French Prime Minister Pflimlin opposed the generals and asked for a parliamentary vote of confidence: the vote had the support of 274 deputies, but 129 deputies voted against the prime minister's rejection of the generals' rule. Pflimlin, not wanting to risk civil war, allowed the government to collapse completely after de Gaulle announced that he was prepared to resume power (Price 1993, 317).

The Algerian-based generals who orchestrated the bloodless coup d'état that ended the Fourth Republic and the vast majority of politicians put their trust in Charles de Gaulle to create a new government. Charles de Gaulle believed that the weakness of the Fourth Republic lay with its parliamentary system, and thus, when given the opportunity to create a new government and constitution, he set out to institute a strong presidential system along the lines of the 1946 Bayeux program he had authored.[10]

De Gaulle believed strongly in the need for the people of France not only to grant their legitimacy to his policies but also to him personally as their leader. Where de Gaulle's belief in the role of popular sovereignty ended and his desire to diminish the influence of the political parties begins is unclear. Charles de Gaulle possessed a coherent political philosophy that, while recognizing the essential role of political parties in democracy, never truly embraced parliamentary politics (Lacouture 1991, 203). Except for the Algerian crisis, de Gaulle's agenda during his tenure in office in the Fifth Republic can be characterized as an effort to strengthen the executive and devolve power away from the legislative institutions of the state.

September 1958 Referendum to Approve the Constitution

De Gaulle's constitution of 1958 took the first step in instituting a stronger presidential form of government and his use of the referendum device to legitimize it would set the precedent for every major decision to come during his tenure. The president retained from the 1946 Fourth Republic Constitution the power to appoint the prime minister who in turn named the rest of the cabinet. The 1958 Constitution symbolically juxtaposed the definition of the powers of the president of the Republic with the introductory definition of sovereignty unlike the 1946 Constitution that defined the office four chapters later. Under the 1946 Constitution, the president was elected solely by members of Parliament; the 1958 Constitution broadened the presidential electoral college to include nearly 80,000 local *notables* that diluted the Parliament's influence. It allowed for the president to call a referendum on public affairs as long as the proposal was made by the government or both assemblies, or chambers, of Parliament. Because the prime minister was appointed by the president, referendum proposals were usually a simple formality.

Another innovation of the 1958 Constitution enabled the president to dissolve the National Assembly after consultation with the prime minister and the two assemblies. This new constitution also granted the president "exceptional powers when the institutions of the Republic, the independence of the nation, the integrity of its territory or the fulfillment of its international obligations were threatened."[11]

The 1958 Constitution reduced the power of Parliament from the constitution of the Fourth Republic. The Parliament remained two-chambered with the National Assembly being retained from the Fourth Republic. The Council of the Republic was scratched and replaced with the Senate, an institution heralding from the Third Republic. Nevertheless, the power of Parliament was limited to legislative and budgetary functions. Even though the government was put more directly under Parliament's control than it had been in the Fourth Republic, the National Assembly could only force the government to disband if a vote of censure commanded an absolute majority or if a government-initiated vote of confidence failed by an absolute majority, and unlike a similar stipulation in the 1946 Constitution, it seemed as if this rule would be followed. Not only were deputies "no longer allowed to introduce measures reducing public resources or increasing public expenditure," but they also had no control over the dates of their sessions or their timetables (Berstein 1993, 10). Thus, the legislature would not control its agenda or its sessions.

The referendum vote on September 28, 1958 recorded an overwhelming victory for de Gaulle and the new constitution despite being labeled as *Bonapartist* by the Left. The constitution was favored by 79.26 percent of voters with an unusually high turnout of 84.94 percent (Berstein 1993, 15). Thus, a total of 66.42 percent of the entire electorate approved of the constitution while only 17.38 percent voted against it. Every single department of France voted "Yes" for the constitution. This vote in no uncertain terms was a crushing defeat for the Left. The Communist Party and the Union des forces démocratiques (UFD) led the main opposition to the referendum. The UFD was made up of those who had broken with a more established party on the Left for various reasons. However, Gaullists were successfully able to portray the Communist Party as the dominant element of the "No" forces. Moreover, the Gaullists and "Yes" forces were able to saturate the media and the public with their message far outstripping the efforts of the opposition "No" forces. Seventeen of the 23 recognized groups that had access to public financing for the referendum campaign supported the "Yes" forces. Journals and posters for the "Yes" campaign flooded the country while its supporters dominated most of the airtime on television and radio. The coup de grace was given by de Gaulle himself in radio and television appeals that appeared to win over the doubtful (Berstein 1993, 15). Even though this vote laid the groundwork for a much stronger presidency than in the Fourth Republic, de Gaulle would not be satisfied.

January 1961 Referendum on Algerian Self-Determination

It has been written that it is impossible to understand the French referendum of January 1961 without understanding the political circumstances in which de Gaulle found himself (Goguel 1962, 17). The Algerian crisis that de Gaulle had been called back into service to solve was at a standstill at best; in fact, after the peace talks had broken down at Melun, tidings of civil war were once again in the air with the army divided over the issue. De Gaulle found himself embattled from all sides: the Left was unhappy with the economic austerity programs; the Centrists were unhappy with his anti-American, anti-European, and anti–United Nations pronouncements; and the extreme Right was nearly at arms over his peace initiatives toward Algiers (Wright 1978, 147). The generals of the Algerian coup d'état had brought de Gaulle back to power specifically so that he would legitimize the war to keep Algeria under French control. De Gaulle, however at the time, had not decided upon a solution (Berstein 1993, 28–9; Lacouture 1991). If the war could not be won, it seems, he favored allowing Algeria to go its own way. Moreover, de Gaulle seemed to favor what the French people favored, and as they tired of the war, they began to accept the idea of Algerian independence. When de Gaulle came to power in 1958, three-quarters of the French population favored keeping Algeria French. By the time of the January 1961 referendum, a majority was now in favor of Algerian independence. In sum, the French people were tired of the war and simply wanted it to be over (Lacouture 1991, 274). Thus by calling a referendum de Gaulle could solve the crisis by allowing Algeria to have self-determination in the face of right-wing opposition and grant himself legitimacy vis-à-vis his many opponents by going directly to the people.

The Algerian Independence movement, known as the *Front de libération nationale* or FLN, disagreed in principle that Algeria's future should be decided by a vote that included the French; moreover, the FLN wanted de Gaulle to negotiate only with the GPRA, the provisional government of the Algerian Republic. De Gaulle, on the other hand, wanted to open up the negotiations to include other participants in case he could negotiate for a mostly independent Algeria with some links to France. For this reason and because he felt he needed to be granted legitimacy from the French population to take on peace negotiations, he decided to call a referendum on Algerian self-determination.

The French Parliament was more of a nonfactor than a factor in the 1961 referendum campaign and on the issue of Algerian independence in general. Following the adoption of the 1958 Constitution, Parliament was extremely weak while de Gaulle was at the height of his charismatic, authoritarian power between 1958 and 1962 (Frears 1977, 15–22).[12] Even though elements within the Parliament and in society in general were against Algerian independence in the beginning, Parliamentary opponents were never able to articulate successfully their political position or form a cohesive coalition; thus the military became the most significant opposition (Berstein 1993, 38–9). Public opinion began to shift in favor of Algerian independence much earlier than the opinion of the parties and individuals within Parliament; therefore, de Gaulle was able to take advantage of the relative policy positions of these actors in 1960. De Gaulle was able to win a referendum vote in January 1961 by capturing a majority of those voting as public opinion crept closer to his position and away from that of Parliament and the political parties.

De Gaulle's appeal to the electorate on behalf of the referendum two days before the vote is the clearest example from his regime of his personal need to connect with the people (Wright 1978, 147). On January 6 de Gaulle made the following pronouncement: "*Françaises, Français*, as you know, your answer is addressed to me. I need, yes, I need to know what is in your hearts and minds. That is why I turn to you above all intermediaries. The matter really is—who does not know it?—between each of you and me" (Lacouture 1991, 274). With 76.5 percent of the electorate turning out in France and Algeria, de Gaulle won the referendum convincingly with 75.3 percent of those voting supporting the concept of Algerian self-determination (Williams 1970, 292). In Algeria itself, 18 percent voted against self-determination but in Algiers City 72 percent voted against the referendum. This latter figure represented the high concentration of Europeans in Algiers City and underlined the necessity of going around the European population of Algiers that was dead set against Algeria leaving French control. The situation was further complicated by the fact that Muslim Algeria was not necessarily of one accord: the FLN had asked for the Muslim population to boycott the vote, which led to a 42 percent abstention in Algeria.

The January 1961 French vote on Algeria illustrates at least one lesson on referendum votes in general: the people's position on issues is often closer to the position of the executive than to the position of those groups with which the executive is competing for power. In this situation, the individuals and parties within and outside of Parliament oriented against Algerian self-determination and de Gaulle steadily lost ground to de Gaulle. More accurately, even though a majority of the population was in favor of a French Algeria in 1958, French public opinion began to shift toward the idea of Algerian independence from 1958 to 1961. De Gaulle was able to strategically position himself to take advantage of this shift in French public opinion. Though the French Parliament also began to shift its views, it had already lost the political initiative and thus de Gaulle was able to record a political victory.

April 1962 Referendum on the Agreement with Algiers

During the winter of 1960–1961 and especially after the January 8 referendum vote, opponents of Algerian independence increased their violent resistance. Civilian and military activists formed a clandestine paramilitary group called the *Organisation armée secrète*, or OAS, in order to resist by force any attempt by the French government to negotiate with the FLN. Besides carrying out attacks on those it suspected of supporting the FLN, it also published its first manifestos in February 1961. The immediate threat came from a group of military officers who had decided to instigate a putsch: most prominently Colonels Argoud, Broziat, Lacheroy, Godard, and Gardes. The rough idea was to bring over the French Algerian army to the mainland to force the political authorities to drop the idea of an independent Algeria and to force de Gaulle to resign. The colonels asked General Challe, commander in chief of Allied forces in central Europe, to lead the effort because they believed only he had the standing to succeed at the effort. He was backed by General André Zeller, former chief of the general staff, and General Jouhard, the former chief of the Algerian air force. The putsch began the night of April 21 with the landing of paratroopers in Algiers and the arrest of General Gambiez, overall commander, General Vezinet, commander of the ground forces, and the Algiers police chief. Others detained included the French Minister of Public Works who happened to be visiting at the time. The ruling military junta crystallized into Generals Challe, Zeller, Jouhard, and Salan, and they conducted their operation so strictly that they excluded and refused contact with their logical allies among the European civilian activists and the OAS (Berstein 1993).

Moreover, support for the putsch outside of the OAS and the European population of Algeria ranged from nearly nonexistent in France to minimal among various military units inside of Algeria. Within France, political forces were nearly unified in their vocal denunciation of the putsch; only the *Centre national des indépendants et paysans* (CNIP) gave its silent approval. Though French public opinion was solidly against the putsch, speeches by Prime Minister Debré and de Gaulle served further to rally the population. In fact, de Gaulle may have given his finest, and certainly his most effective, speech ever on the night of April 23 denouncing the generals; scholars have noted that this speech isolated the members of the putsch and became the turning point in the crisis (Berstein 1993, 50; Lacouture 1991, 284):

An insurrectional power has been set up in Algeria by a military junta.

This power has an appearance, a quartet of retired generals. It has a reality: a group of partisan, ambitious, fanatical officers. This group and that quartet possess a certain expeditious and limited skill. But they see and understand the nation and the world only through their distorted frenzy. Their enterprise is leading straight to national disaster. The State is flouted, the nation defied, our power shaken, our international prestige abashed, our place and our role in Africa comprised. And by whom? Alas! Alas! By men whose duty, honour, raison d'être is to serve and obey.

In the name of France, I order that every means, I say every means, be used to close the road to those men, until they are crushed. I forbid any Frenchman and, above all, any soldier to carry out any of their orders. The only leaders, civil and military, who have the right to assume responsibilities are those who have been properly appointed to do so. The future of the usurpers must only be the one that destines them to the full rigour of the law.

So that the misfortune that hovers over the nation and the threat that weighs over the Republic can be alleviated, I have decided to implement article 16 of our Constitution, having taken official advice from the Constitutional Council, the Prime Minister, the President of the Senate, and the President of the National Assembly. From today, if necessary directly, I shall take whatever steps seem to me to be required by the circumstances. I hereby declare, for today and for tomorrow, that I shall maintain the French and republican legitimacy that the nation has conferred upon me, whatever happens, to the full term of my mandate or until such time as I lack the strength or life to do so, and I shall take every means possible to ensure that it remains after me. French men and women, see the course that France runs the risk of going and compare it

with what was beginning once again. French men and women, help me!
(De Gaulle 1970, III, 306–8)

De Gaulle's appeal swayed the already uncertain military to his side
and led to the collapse of the coup d'état within hours. Many of the rank
and file soldiers defied the orders of the putschists while the officers,
who were hesitant to take sides in the first place, were now resolved to
stay out of the conflict. The air force in Algeria flew back to the mainland to be out of the putschists' reach. The rebellious generals only had
the support of the European population in Algiers, and because they had
only conceived of a military action, they were not prepared or inclined
to lead a civil uprising. On April 24, two days after de Gaulle's speech,
Generals Challe and Zeller surrendered along with most of the para-
chutists while Generals Salan and Jouhard went underground and joined
the OAS.

It soon became evident after the failed coup d'état that the only
solution to the crisis was Algerian independence. Throughout the peace
negotiations that had begun after the January 1961 referendum, the
FLN was uncompromising in its demands; eventually over the months
to come the French negotiating team and de Gaulle conceded to the
FLN everything it wanted. Even though the FLN had been guilty of
terrorism throughout its existence, in April 1961, 78 percent of the
French citizenry approved of the negotiations with the FLN while
57 percent believed that they would end in Algerian independence
(Berstein 1993, 53). The terrorist and murderous actions of the OAS,
including an assassination attempt on de Gaulle himself in September
1961, only served to bolster French public opinion against extending
the conflict. The intensity of the situation was further heightened by the
Left's denunciation of OAS violence and its calls for peace. Despite an
official ban, trade unions organized several mass demonstrations of over
15,000 people in Paris. During one of these demonstrations in February
1962, eight people died after a police charge in a metro station. In short,
both internal and external challenges to the integrity of the state had
developed into a "virtual civil war" that demanded an end to the conflict
(Berstein 1993, 53). France and Algeria took the first steps toward
Algerian independence on March 18, 1962 with the signing of the Evian
agreement; the next day the provisional government of the Republic of
Algeria called for the cessation of hostilities.

De Gaulle called for a referendum to be held in France on April 8,
1962 to ratify the agreement and give him the authority to implement
its provisions. Every political party throughout the ideological spectrum

supported the referendum vote except for two. The *Parti socialiste unifié* (PSU) advocated that its members write in "Yes to peace, no to Gaullist power." The CNIP's decision to give no advice to its members was interpreted as it being against the vote. An overwhelming 90.6 percent of those voting supported the referendum with 75.6 percent of the electorate participating in France (Williams 1970, 292); it should be noted that Algerian residents did not participate in this vote. Given the desire of the French people to see an end to the conflict, however, the overwhelming support for the referendum was understandable.

However, was it necessary to call the April 1962 referendum? Public opinion had been solidly on de Gaulle's side for a few years and even most political parties by 1962 supported the idea of Algerian independence. Therefore it may not have been politically necessary to call the vote. Moreover, there was no legal necessity to have the people ratify the agreement with Algiers. It seems as if this referendum vote was necessary from de Gaulle's perspective in order to satisfy his personal need to be regularly legitimized by the public's vote. The one general lesson that can be taken from the April 1962 French referendum is that groups other than a legislature, like the military, can compete with the executive for power in the context of referendum politics.

Though Algeria did gain its independence, it did so in a way that disappointed many of the hopes of the Evian agreement. The OAS decided to disrupt the implementation of the peace agreement and Algerian independence at all costs. When it attempted to turn part of Algiers city into an armed rebel camp and disarm the French soldiers in the area, the insurrection was put down with a massive military force that included tanks and planes. Afterwards the OAS became even more desperate leading to ever-increasing levels of killing and terror. Finally it reached the point at which the European and Muslim populations of Algeria could no longer live side by side. The European population realized that once independence had been fully gained, it would be open to reprisals for all the horror the OAS had visited upon the Muslim population. The arrest of Generals Jouhard and Salan, Salan's life sentence, and Jouhard's execution finally forced the OAS to enter into negotiations with the provisional Algerian government. With the end of the OAS near, hundreds of thousands of European Algerians emigrated to mainland France, Spain, and Israel. The Europeans who were left along with the Muslim population were nearly unanimous in their approval of Algerian independence: 99.72 percent of the electorate in Algeria voted for the country's independence in a referendum on July 1 (Berstein 1993, 56). With de Gaulle's formal recognition of independence on

July 3, Algeria finally became sovereign over its affairs and the Algerian chapter in French history was finally closed. The Algerian conflict had dominated political life within France for years and was responsible for the return of de Gaulle himself. Now that the conflict was over, de Gaulle turned inwards toward his goals regarding France.

The Distribution of Power Between the French President and Parliament and the Last Two Gaullist Referendums

The last two referendums called by de Gaulle also go very far in illustrating how leaders may use the referendum device to attempt to defeat their opponents (Wright 1978, 148). The October 1962 vote for the direct election of the president in France increased the legitimacy of that institution while decreasing that of the Parliament. The 1969 referendum vote to devolve power away from the Senate was in some ways a blatant attempt by de Gaulle to destroy the institutional basis of his political enemies. Both of these referendums serve as excellent examples of how referendums can change the distribution of power between institutions and the visceral response they invoke from their opponents.

In the battle between de Gaulle and Parliament, de Gaulle clearly had the power to go to the people; the people could only legitimize a policy or institutional change if *asked*. The referendum gave de Gaulle added power to see his goals fulfilled. The power of the referendum device in these cases is illustrated by the fact that the president of France is now elected directly by the French people. Though the people were the deciding factor in the referendum vote, de Gaulle, an executive leader, decided whether or not the votes would be held. The French electorate sided with de Gaulle on the direct election of the president but went against his wish to devolve power away from the Senate. De Gaulle was well aware of the people's sentiment in the latter vote but decided to hold it anyway.

October 1962 Referendum on the Direct Election of the President

De Gaulle's referendum proposal on the direct election of the president by the people instead of by the legislature ordained him as the *ne plus ultra* political strategist of the French Fifth Republic. Though he would later stumble in his referendum attempt to devolve power away from the Senate, this referendum, his fourth use of direct democracy in his tenure, at once solidified de Gaulle as the master populist democrat and manipulator of the rules of the game. No single move encapsuled his philosophy, goals, and tactics more completely. In one move, he accomplished three significant goals. If the issue came to a vote and the people decided in favor of the direct election of the president, Parliament's power with regards to the president would be severely diminished. Second, de Gaulle would succeed at his omnipresent goal of attaining on a regular basis the approval of the people not only for his policies but also particularly for his personal leadership. Third, de Gaulle would be hailed as a democrat for his desire to empower the people with such an important decision. De Gaulle first referred to this upcoming proposal in a June 8, 1962 television broadcast: "Between the People and Him who is entrusted with its government there must be, in the modern world of our Republic, a direct bond. When the time is right we will need to ensure through universal suffrage that in future the Republic may remain strong, organized and permanent—even though its leaders are mortal" (De Gaulle 1970, III, 422–3; Berstein 1993, 71). The decision to hold the referendum was made at a Council of Ministers meeting on September 12, 1962. With one move, de Gaulle could accomplish all of his goals.

Parliamentarians and members of France's political parties denounced de Gaulle's proposal with extreme venom and near-perfect unanimity. Only the *Union pour la nouvelle république* (UNR) failed to denounce de Gaulle's proposal. From the parliamentarians' perspective, de Gaulle's proposal was a direct assault upon their sovereignty and the true nature of the political state. Most parliamentarians viewed the French state as one being dominated by a legislative form of government whose members were voted on and received their legitimacy from the people (Berstein 1993, 72). In fact, whether France had a presidential or parliamentary governmental system had been a question since the institution of the Gaullist constitution of 1958. The political parties knew that once de Gaulle had secured the popular election of the president, the legitimacy and power of Parliament would become secondary. Therefore the parties united against de Gaulle and his referendum in order to defend traditional republicanism based upon parliamentary rule.

Jurists and specialists on constitutional matters also decried de Gaulle's proposal as wrong-headed on procedural grounds. They claimed that amending the constitution required the use of article 89, which stated "a governmental or parliamentary proposal of constitutional revision must be voted in identical form by both Assemblies. It enters into application once it has been approved by referendum" (Berstein 1993, 72). De Gaulle had invoked article 11, which they countered by arguing that it only applied to "ordinary, and not to constitutional, laws" (Berstein 1993, 72). In this way, many jurists were in the ironic position of arguing the intent and meaning of the constitution to the one person—de Gaulle—most responsible for its composition; their arguments could not help but be hurt by that fact. De Gaulle responded to their arguments snidely by saying that it was "real impertinence to presume to challenge [him] on its meaning" (De Gaulle 1970, II, 29).

The Parliament voted to censure de Gaulle and his government with 280 votes—39 more votes than the necessary majority to do so—on October 5. It had reconvened on October 2 and was immediately presented with a formal message from de Gaulle stating that the referendum would take place at the end of the month. In the National Assembly, the motion voted upon demanded the censure of the government—the prime minister et al.—based on the argument that de Gaulle could only call the referendum if the prime minister had put forth the proposal. Paul Reynaud expressed the sentiment of the Parliament when he said, "For us republicans, France exists here and nowhere else. . . . The representatives of the people assembled together constitute the Nation and there can be no more solemn declaration of the People's will than the vote which they take after public deliberation" (Berstein 1993, 73). De Gaulle responded by dissolving the National Assembly, keeping the government in office, and ordering new legislative elections after the referendum on November 18 and 25, 1962.

Though the persons arrayed against the referendum were many, de Gaulle still enjoyed the upper hand in the upcoming vote. The electorate would have to choose between the traditional republican political culture of France that equated the republic with the Parliament, and the warmth and assurance of De Gaulle's leadership. The former had fallen out of favor since the failure of these parliamentarian institutions in the Fourth Republic. On the other hand de Gaulle's leadership, though often paternalistic, satisfied a desire within the French to be led (Berstein 1993, 75). De Gaulle also sold the "Yes" vote for the referendum as a chance for the electorate to give itself the right to choose the president itself. And once again, de Gaulle threatened to resign if the electorate did not support his referendum: "If you reject my proposal and follow the advice of the old parties who want to restore their disastrous regime and of all the subversives who seek an outlet for their sedition; or if the majority you grant me is feeble, mediocre and indecisive, then it goes without saying that my task will be immediately—and irrevocably—ended" (De Gaulle 1970, *Discours et messages*, IV, 36). This referendum vote became the defining moment for the French Fifth

Republic because its decision would define the institutional nature of the regime. Failure to pass the referendum would endorse returning to the parliamentarism of the Fourth Republic while a positive vote would institutionalize the presidentialism that de Gaulle had crafted the French regime into.

On October 28, the French electorate chose to support de Gaulle and the direct election of the president by a majority vote though it was smaller than the 1958 vote for the constitution. In 1958 there was a 15 percent absentee rate while in this vote the percentage of absentees was 22.76. Although the "Yes" vote won with 61.75 percent of those voting, that percentage of the vote only represented 46.44 percent of the electorate—less than a majority (Williams 1970, 292). In 1958, the "Yes" vote for the constitution won with 79.26 percent of those voting, which translated into 66.42 percent of the electorate. The decreased support of the electorate indicated the extent of public anxiety over the choice that de Gaulle had given them (Berstein 1993, 77). Nevertheless, the Gaullist reading of the constitution prevailed and this referendum victory haunted the parliamentary elections scheduled for less than a month later.

In a speech on November 7, de Gaulle framed the upcoming parliamentary elections on November 18 and 25 as a choice between "yesterday's parties" and the "new Republic" (Berstein 1993, 78); the public seems to have been listening. The Gaullists—the UNR and the UDT—won 31.9 percent of the votes cast in the first round, a landslide. After the second round, the Gaullists had 233 seats, nine short of an absolute majority. With the addition of Valéry Giscard d'Estaing's 36 independent Republicans, the Gaullists had a solid majority in Parliament that shattered the traditional party system (Berstein 1993, 79–80).

Thus, by late 1962, de Gaulle had achieved much of what he desired politically for France. He had established a semi-presidential system of government through the 1958 referendum on the Constitution and the October 1962 referendum on the direct election of the president. Moreover, he had defeated the parties he felt were responsible for the problematic Fourth Republic. In doing so he changed forever the French party system. The direct election of the president changed the political calculus; parties in France knew now that they had to reform or die. They needed to compete for the presidency as well as parliament in order to give themselves the opportunity to wield maximum power. De Gaulle had fundamentally changed the French political landscape and it was believed that his power and influence had reached its pinnacle. Ironically, however, it was the Gaullist, parliamentary majority that came to power after 1962 that began to challenge de Gaulle's singular, personal hold on political legitimacy (Frears 1977, 23).

Moreover, the last referendum that de Gaulle would call showed that no one is immune from the inevitable change that takes place within a polity. Though in an objective sense the French people were doing well economically, they felt as if they were no better or worse as time passed. The French people had high expectations concerning their economic, social, and international political status that began to outflank de Gaulle's ability to stay ahead of their desires. Eventually, de Gaulle would prove to be out of step with a majority of the French population and become, inconceivable in 1962 but quite obvious in 1968, an anachronism that the French would believe whose time had passed.

April 1969 Referendum on Devolution of Power from the Senate and Regional Reform

Signs and portents of de Gaulle's future weakness were evident from the presidential campaign of 1965. Most assumed that de Gaulle would win the first direct election for president handily with little to no opposition. De Gaulle had proven himself to be the master politician and had defeated not only the parties but also the party system just three years before. His penchant for wanting to connect with the people would only help him in his campaign for president. In hindsight, of course, it is quite obvious that expectations for de Gaulle were very high and that anything but a resounding win in the first round might be considered a defeat. As it turns out, de Gaulle did not receive a majority of the vote in the first round and was forced to a second-round vote on December 5, 1965.

De Gaulle faced two strong opposition candidates in François Mitterrand of the Center-Left and Left, and Jean Lecanuet of the Center-Right and Right. Mitterrand campaigned on a platform of social justice while Lecanuet focused upon three themes—democracy, social responsiveness, and an appreciation for the "European" concept. These themes were aimed at de Gaulle's perceived weaknesses—his authoritarianism, indifference to social problems, and excessively nationalistic posturing with regards to Europe (Berstein 1993, 195). The unprecedented appeal these candidates had through the medium of television combined with the appeal of their relative youth—Mitterrand was 49, Lecanuet was 45, and de Gaulle was 75!—began to show itself in public opinion polls and forced de Gaulle actually to campaign. Though François Mitterrand's gains in public opinion polls were significant—he rose from 23 to

27 percent—the gains by Jean Lecanuet were amazing. Lecanuet rose from 5 percent of those being polled to 20 percent, a gain of 15 percent, mostly at de Gaulle's expense because of their appeal to the same voters (Berstein 1993, 197). These gains, however, did not translate into a run-off spot for Lecanuet, who only received 15.9 percent of the vote on election day, but it did give confidence to opposition in the Center-Right and Right that it could organize and unite. Mitterrand, on the other hand, won 32.3 percent of the vote after de Gaulle's 43.7 percent and earned himself the opportunity to face de Gaulle in a second-round run-off.

Though de Gaulle prevailed in the second round and was elected president of France, the election cast doubt on his invincibility and his hold on the pulse of the French polity. In actuality, he gained votes over the coalition of parties that represented Gaullism in the last parliamentary elections winning 13 departments with an absolute majority and 70 more with a plurality of votes (Berstein 1993, 200). In the end, those voters who had supported Lecanuet would not cast their vote for the candidate of the united Left. Thus, de Gaulle won 54.5 percent of the vote while Mitterrand won 45.5 percent. Nevertheless, the fact that de Gaulle had been forced into a second round signaled to some that de Gaulle was truly unpopular with a significant proportion of the population based not only upon his social and international policies but also because of his paternalism. Because this was an election more about personalities than parties, de Gaulle's personal legitimacy took something of a blow from being forced into a second-round election even though he prevailed. And, perhaps most significantly, the opposition camps on the Left and the Right gained both positive electoral experience and confidence.

The 1967 parliamentary elections showed further signs of weakness in the Gaullist hold on power. Though the first round of elections were consistent with public opinion polling that had been done, the second round proved to be something of a shock. In the first round, Gaullists won 37.7 percent of the vote as had been predicted; 37.7 percent, in fact, was their highest ever percentage of the vote (Berstein 1993, 206). But in the second round the Gaullists relinquished so much ground that they nearly lost their majority status. Of the 470 mainland seats, Gaullists only won 233; overall seat totals including the overseas vote gave the Gaullists 247 seats as opposed to the 240 seats of the opposition. This electoral result had several explanations. First, Gaullists may have been too complacent in getting out the vote after receiving a strong first-round vote. Second, Centrists may have voted for the opposition out of concern for how Gaullists might have interpreted an overwhelming victory. Last, it should be noted that the electoral pact between the socialists and communists worked extremely well. Understanding that the electorate probably would not choose a communist in the final analysis, many vote-leading communist candidates stepped aside and endorsed the socialist candidate (Berstein 1993, 207).

The May 1968 crisis in France—a general "malaise" defined mostly by student and labor unrest—thoroughly permeated French society and challenged its leaders to find a solution (Bertier de Sauvigny and Pinkney 1983, 389–90). A solution was particularly difficult given that the crisis concerned "quality of life" issues that were not readily addressed through any kind of institutional reforms. In short, robust economic growth created a backlash against consumerism and the values it projected along with a general backlash against tradition and authority present among students in the United States, Europe, and Asia. The exponential growth of the number of students in higher education in France was also a contributing factor. The crisis began with students at the University of Paris at Nanterre—a newly constructed campus far from the center of Paris or any urban life—who had been experiencing overcrowding in the university dorm and class room, and who also feared not finding work upon graduation. Campus protests and sit-in's soon spread to spontaneous, undirected labor unrest throughout the country on May 13. By the time labor leaders jumped on the bandwagon by calling for strikes on May 16, many local trade unions had already called strikes on their own.

The initial ineffective response of the political system to student and labor unrest revealed its weaknesses. For a while, political authorities discounted the seriousness of these events and attempted to ignore them. Prime Minister Georges Pompidou left Paris for a ten-day trip to Afghanistan on May 2—the day the Nanterre campus was closed by its dean. Within a day the students from Nanterre arrived at the Sorbonne's campus in Paris. Brutal police action against the Nanterre students not only cemented their solidarity with the students at the Sorbonne but its continuance on the night of May 10—the "night of the barricade"— won over the sympathy of the people. Up until then, the public at large had been wary of the student uprising but it now began to embrace it. De Gaulle decided to go ahead with an official visit to Romania on May 14 even though the unrest had just spread to the trade unions and Pompidou's attempts at compromise with the students at the Sorbonne had fallen short days before (Berstein 1993, 215–16).

After his return, de Gaulle responded to the growing labor unrest by proposing on May 24, 1968, a referendum that would give the head of state, that is himself, the authority to "change wherever necessary outdated and rigid structures" (Berstein 1993, 218). Theoretically, this proposal may have succeeded in meeting some of the demands of those fermenting unrest, but in fact it was a complete failure. In truth de Gaulle was asking the people to empower not themselves but an exec-utive who would fix their grievances as he saw fit. His speech proposing the vote sounded like "a piece of eighteenth-century prose in a surreal-ist meeting" compared to the revolutionary rhetoric of the activists (Lacouture 1991, 538).

Other proposed solutions also failed in the upcoming days. Prime Minister Pompidou concluded a set of negotiations with labor leaders on May 27 whose offerings did not satisfy the striking workers. The UNEF—*Union nationale des étudiants de France*—and the PSU—*Parti socialiste unifé*—offered revolution as a solution; however, the revolution the students and workers had been advocating for weeks did not possess any plan for what would happen after various institutions had been dissolved. On May 28 François Mitterrand proposed a provisional govern-ment of ten men, and new presidential and parliamentary elections. The Communist Party (PCF) called for a vague "popular government." The failure of French leaders to find a political solution to the country's social problems had finally brought about an extremely serious political crisis (Berstein 1993, 220).

Then, surprisingly, de Gaulle simply took control. He gave a speech on May 30 in which he said that because a communist coup might be near he would reassert the authority of the state through several initia-tives: Prime Minister Pompidou would remain in office despite calls for his resignation even by some independent republicans; new elections would be held for the National Assembly; and he pledged to use all of the powers given to him by the constitution if necessary to maintain order. The French polity responded to de Gaulle's moves with great and unexpected approval. It was clear that the people at large were growing tired of the uncertainty and chaos of the past month; marches and demonstrations continued but they were now pro-government and pro-order rallies alongside pro-revolution ones. In fact, public opinion began to move against those activists who advocated revolution as their calls for continuing the strikes and participation in violent demonstrations began to diminish their legitimacy (Berstein 1993, 221–2).

The June 1968 election for Parliament was a landslide for the Gaullist majority who campaigned on a platform that emphasized order and attacked what they called a "communist plot." In fact, the Communist Party had done everything it could to halt the social crisis in May having identified its leaders among the students and in labor as those with views it did not share. Nevertheless, it was easy for the Gaullists to label the social uprising as a "communist plot" and therefore scare the electorate into supporting them. In this way the June 1968 election was vastly simplified and presented a distinct advantage to the ruling majority. Only the *Parti socialiste unifé* (PSU) campaigned on a platform similar to what the May Crisis had advocated. The Communist Party and the *Fédération de la gauche démocratique et socialiste* (FGDS) both ran traditional campaigns that called for reforms within the system through constitutional and legal means. The electorate was also voting out of fear of disorder. The demonstrations, riots, and strikes scared even those who participated in them; no one wanted to see a total melt-down of society take place. In the election, the UDR won an overall majority with 293 seats; this was the first time any one group had ever achieved a majority independently. The entire Gaullist block garnered 354 out of 487, or 75 percent of the seats in Parliament. One side effect, though, of this parliamentary landslide was that many conservative deputies had been chosen by an electorate that was presently frightened of disorder.

De Gaulle, on the other hand, had not forgotten about his failed referendum proposal of May 24. De Gaulle still possessed a personal need to reaffirm his mandate from the people through universal suffrage; even though his party had unprecedented success in the June 1968 elections, he knew the success was not mostly due to his efforts. The success of the Gaullists in the June 1968 elections had everything to do with Georges Pompidou and his leadership; in fact, this may be the reason de Gaulle fired Pompidou in a surprise move (Lacouture 1991, 561–2).[13] As de Gaulle believed that the people of France yearned for ways to participate in their own governance, his reform efforts focused upon the concept of participation. De Gaulle promoted both university and regional reform, but it was only the latter that became controversial. Moreover, only regional reform became the topic of the referendum he so desperately needed to call.

Regional reform encompassed not only the development of regional councils but also a reformation of the Senate that stripped it of all legislative powers. Both the regional councils and the Senate had served as bastions of the opposition, de Gaulle's political enemies, since 1958. This reform was controversial because it would strip both sets of insti-tutions, and therefore de Gaulle's enemies, of power. The members of the new regional councils, who mostly consisted of anti-Gaullist local notables, would no longer be elected; members would be appointed by various economic, social, and cultural institutions (Hayward 1969, 291). Under de Gaulle's reforms, the Senate would become a simple consultative body with no role or responsibility whatsoever in governing. Modeled on the new regional councils, the Senate's membership would be made up of 173 representatives chosen on a regional basis by an electoral college and 146 representatives chosen by the national offices of various economic, social, and cultural associations (Berstein 1993, 232). Not one of the new senators would be elected directly by the people. The new Senate's role would be to give advice to the National Assembly on bills, but it was advice that the National Assembly could completely ignore.

Why de Gaulle continued to pursue the devolution of power away from the Parliament and the Senate in particular after 1962 may not seem reasonable. He had defeated and weakened the Parliament in significant ways. The Gaullists, moreover, had achieved unprecedented electoral success in Parliament. It should be remembered, though, that de Gaulle had blamed the troubles of the Fourth Republic squarely upon Parliament; he had always been a staunch opponent of the institution. Though de Gaulle had been searching for a referendum topic that would allow him seek the approval of the people, it is fair to argue that he also wanted to see further harm done to the Senate. One detail of the reforms he proposed highlights this argument: the president of the Senate would no longer be next in line as chief executive if something were to happen to the president; the prime minister would now be next in line for succession (Berstein 1993, 233). The French people, however, interpreted this referendum as de Gaulle's desire to extinguish his political enemies and not as a means for themselves to participate in government.

This referendum proposal generated little support among the population while the political coalition allied against de Gaulle's referendum was enormous. De Gaulle's attempt to connect with the people in a positive way through this upcoming vote did not succeed. The social discontent that was present in the May 1968 crisis had simply been swept underneath the rug. Various economic policies of de Gaulle's administration served to spur on several constituencies. A decision by the government to hold down wages as a mechanism to fight inflation had recently upset the trade unions. Economic growth challenged many uncompetitive, small businesses to modernize and otherwise keep up. Larger firms and businesses were upset with the state monetary policy dictated more by national politics than economic sense. Discontent threatened the majority that had voted in de Gaulle and the Gaullists;

the most vocal of these were the independent republicans who had been excluded from the government since 1966 (Berstein 1993, 235). Even though de Gaulle threatened to resign as usual if the referendum was not supported, this time the electorate and especially the majority that had supported Gaullism in the past could look forward to Georges Pompidou as a replacement for de Gaulle.

Though Pompidou had dutifully supported de Gaulle in the referendum campaign, he also worked to increase his own personal status. Having been fired as prime minister gave him the opportunity to put some distance between himself and de Gaulle. Joining the referendum campaign immediately revived the significant public image he had acquired from the May 1968 crisis and June 1968 parliamentary elections he marshaled. And even though he had been asked by de Gaulle's henchmen to announce that he would not be considered a candidate for president in case de Gaulle stepped down, he would never make such an announcement. In fact, he had famously announced in Rome back on January 18, 1969 that he would be a candidate for the presidency once it became vacant (Hayward 1969, 311). Therefore the Gaullists and their supporters in the electorate perceived Pompidou as a safety net that allowed them to vote their conscience more easily on the Senate reform referendum.

De Gaulle lost the referendum with 53.2 percent voting "No" (Williams 1970, 292). For this vote 80.6 percent of the electorate turned out; only the 1958 vote to approve the Constitution had a higher referendum turnout with 84.94 percent (Berstein 1993, 15). Polling done before the referendum showed a clear progression of the electorate toward rejecting the measure (Berstein 1993, 237). De Gaulle had lost 71 departments; only 24 had voted "Yes" (Berstein 1993, 238). On April 28, 1969, he released the statement that announced his resignation: "I am ceasing to exercise my functions as President of the Republic. This decision takes effect at noon today."[14]

De Gaulle, so desirous of public approval, had chosen to exit from the political stage with a very public and very dramatic referendum vote. De Gaulle had suspected that the referendum would end in defeat for months. He seemed resigned to allow the referendum result to decide whether or not he would remain in the presidency as he had proclaimed he would since the first popular vote in 1958. In this way he chose his exit from the political stage. André Malraux proposed the idea of the "referendum as suicide" suggesting that de Gaulle wanted the people to demonstrate the connection between himself and France on a topic so unpalatable that a positive vote would prove their "love" for him beyond measure (Lacouture 1991, 572–3; Hayward 1969).

In summary, the French referendums of the Fifth Republic under de Gaulle illustrate many important points that will reoccur throughout this work. First, these French referendums were not the same because they did not have the same subject matter. The 1958, October 1962, and 1969 referendums all dealt with the distribution of power between state institutions—they are *constitutional* referendums by my definition. The 1961 and April 1962 referendums concerned Algerian independence and thus can be considered *autonomy* referendums. Second, powerful leaders who favor presidential systems use the referendum device to increase their own power. Third, sometimes the ego of a leader may cause him or her to underestimate the chance of losing a vote.

Referendums in Chile in Pinochet's Shadow

Political authorities have proposed and/or called at least six referendums in Chile in the twentieth century; since the 1973 military coup that left President Salvador Allende dead, four of these referendums have been held. On August 30, 1925 Chileans voted to approve their constitution with 94.7 percent of the vote and 86.3 percent turnout. On September 11, 1973 Salvador Allende was to announce an upcoming referendum on the approval of the *Área de propiedad social* (the socialized sector of the economy). On January 4, 1978 a vote was held to approve Pinochet's defense of Chile's human rights record in the face of a U.N. resolution denouncing the military regime's abuses; officially 78.4 percent of Chileans approved with a turnout of 91.4 percent. On September 11, 1980, Chileans approved of a new constitution where officially 69.0 percent voted in approval with 92.9 percent turnout. On October 5, 1988, the Chilean people turned down a vote that would have extended Pinochet's term as president without holding an election with 57.0 percent voting against it. On July 30, 1989 the Chilean people once again approved a new constitution with 85.7 percent voting in approval (Butler and Ranney 1994; Oppenheim 1993).

The anti-Communist military junta that came to power in 1973 has been simultaneously denounced for its despicable human rights record while applauded by others for its economic reforms that have, relative to other Latin American countries, been a success. It has never, however, been able to claim legitimacy through the popular support of a majority of the people. General Augusto Pinochet consolidated his power as head of the junta and held referendum votes in 1978 and 1980 that were widely considered to have been fraudulent (Spooner 1994, 153–5; Oppenheim 1993). However, two votes—one proposed under Allende in 1973 and one called under Pinochet in 1988—are of particular interest to this study.

In the last days of the Allende regime, it seemed as if the political stalemate between Allende's party *Unidad Popular* (UP) and the Center-Right and far right would end in violence. The parliamentary elections of March 1973 did not resolve the conflict over the socialization of the economy embodied in the UP's economic program *Área de propiedad social* (APS). Society had become polarized around the issue in the first three years of the Allende regime with opposition growing even at the grass roots level. The October strike of 1972, led by the middle class and owners and thought to have been supported by the CIA, illustrated just how warped the political scene had become (Oppenheim 1993). Sabotage from forces on the Right and further CIA involvement did not help the situation; the CIA's involvement in Chile, along with other U.S. government agencies, is well documented (Kaufman 1988; Sigmund 1977). The UP and its supporters responded with demonstrations of their own and an attempt to find compromise on the APS with the Christian Democratic Party (PDC).

In short, the Chilean polity was hopelessly fragmented between Allende's government and the Right opposition. While Allende was clearly to the Left and the military was clearly to the Right, the people and Parliament were more ambiguous. In the election for president in 1970, the Chilean people were equally divided into Left, Center, and Right political groupings. On the Left, Salvador Allende garnered a plurality of the vote with 36.2 percent. The Center, represented by Radomiro Tomic, garnered 27.8 percent of the vote. Jorge Alessandri represented the Right; he garnered 34.9 percent. Allende's 36.2 percent beat Alessandri's 34.9 percent with a margin of only 39,000 votes out of three million votes cast (Sigmund 1977, 107). The Chilean Parliament contained essentially two factions: Allende's pro-government party UP and the opposition coalition *Confederación Democrática* (CODE); before the election, CODE held majorities in both the upper and lower houses. In the 1973 parliamentary election, CODE won 55.74 percent of the vote while the UP won 43.98 percent. This vote translated into marginally smaller majorities for CODE: 30 out of 50 seats in the Senate, the upper house, and 87 out of 150 in the Chamber, the lower house (Sigmund 1977, 199).

After the attempt at compromise failed with the PDC, Allende came to the conclusion that a referendum was the last best chance to resolve the stalemate in his favor. However there is some discrepancy in the historical record on what the referendum subject would have been. Some have reported that the referendum was to be on the APS and the socialist policy direction in general of the administration (Oppenheim 1993, 84–6). Others have noted that the referendum would have decided whether or not Allende would have continued in office (Sigmund 1977, 239; Kaufman 1988, 296). It seems as if the referendum, irrespective of the formal subject, would in effect decide both Allende's tenure and his policies (Davis 1985, 217). Though Allende did not yet have the support of the Socialist Party, he went ahead with plans to announce the referendum publicly on September 11.[15]

At the time, Pinochet was Allende's military chief and was believed to be loyal. However, it seems that Pinochet indeed was not loyal and used the information against Allende. Allende informed Generals Pinochet and Urbina on September 9 that he would call a referendum "so that the country may decide which way to go"; the generals were astonished on hearing the news (Garcés 1974, 353). The day of the scheduled referendum announcement was the day the coup took place; it had begun early in the morning long before Allende was able to arrive at the presidential palace to make his scheduled noon speech announcing the vote.

Though the referendum proposal was certainly not the cause of the coup, it may be argued that the referendum proposal was the proximate cause, or trigger, of the Chilean coup d'état. Originally the coup had been set for September 14, but Pinochet stated afterwards that the decision to move the coup up to September 11 had been made on the afternoon of September 9—the day he learned from Allende of the upcoming September 11 referendum announcement (Pinochet 1980, 120–3). The military junta decided to begin the coup on the day Allende was to announce the referendum; thus, the referendum proposal may have "hastened the coup" (Oppenheim 1993, 85; Kaufman 1988, 295–6). It has been argued that if the referendum announcement had taken place, it would have been embarrassing for the coup leaders to begin their overthrow of the government while a public vote was pending and thus could have even postponed the coup for several months while the plebiscite was implemented (Kaufman 1988, 295). Therefore moving the time of the coup up may have been a preemptive strike against the referendum and Allende.

The parliamentary opposition to the UP had been advocating a military coup since the March 1973 elections after being united in wanting the UP out of power. The opposition began to lay the groundwork for such a coup by trying to discredit the UP at the mass, elite, and institutional levels (Oppenheim 1993, 79–80). Though tensions were at a crisis level by August 1973 without the referendum, the upcoming referendum proposal may have been the last justification needed to carry out the coup. In this way, the above story provides anecdotal evidence of how a referendum can serve as an intermediate variable that exacerbates a conflictual situation by narrowing the actor's perceptions of the number of options and therefore raising the stakes.

The second referendum vote of interest was held in 1988 to approve or disapprove of General Augusto Pinochet continuing his autocratic rule in the office of president for an additional eight years. Pinochet did not believe he could lose the vote irrespective of polling that had been done beforehand and the warnings of his advisors. Pinochet went on to lose the referendum vote and new elections were held in December 1989 for president and Parliament. Nevertheless, the military junta passed a flurry of laws that tied the hands of the new civilian government and cemented their economic and political system in place for years to come (Oppenheim 1993, 193). Pinochet also continued in his role as head of the armed forces through 1998 delaying democracy's complete come-back in Chile. Nevertheless, the referendum loss is a compelling story of how leaders, even autocratic ones, desire to have the approval of the public even though they wield *de facto* absolute power.

Pinochet had been offered several ways out of the plebiscite vote. He ignored the suggestion to call open elections that might have divided the opposition vote. He also ignored the suggestion to step aside and allow a less controversial civilian candidate to run on the government's economic platform. Instead he attempted to win over the public by cutting taxes, opening new housing projects, and making campaign promises. Chileans, though, could not forget the atrocities he had been ultimately responsible for over the last 15 years; thus Pinochet's campaign proclamations, especially on the merits of democracy, fell on deaf ears. A majority of the Chilean people had begun to move steadily toward the Left and Center-Left under Pinochet's rule. Orlando Saenz, a leading businessman and supporter of the opposition, said of Pinochet, "He suffered the disease of all dictators . . . he started to live in a world of make-believe."[16] It has also been suggested that Pinochet wanted to remain in office because he feared, like dictators faced with stepping down often do, that his and his family's safety might be in jeopardy (Valenzuela and Constable 1988, 29).

The military junta that controlled the armed forces played an interesting role in the plebiscite. Pinochet was not their first choice for president precisely because of his liabilities, and so two members of the junta made their support of him conditional on the referendum campaign and vote actually being conducted freely and fairly.[17] In fact, the members of the junta considered changing the constitution and making the referendum an open election for president (Valenzuela and Constable 1988, 30). General Fernando Matthei of the air force and General Rodolfo Stange of the military police have also been reported as saying that they would encourage Pinochet to step down gracefully if the political situation became chaotic.[18] General Matthei of the air force and Admiral José Toribio Merino of the navy were also reported as being against any kind of coup to suppress the negative referendum results; it seems as if Pinochet was in favor of suspending the referendum but was disallowed by these members of the junta.[19]

The Center-Left and opposition parties effectively organized a campaign against Pinochet that united all of its disparate parts in a way it would never be able to duplicate again. Begun in early 1987, the opposition knew that they would face roadblocks in their campaign. First, the government outlawed all parties that advocated class conflict. This led the communists to ignore the referendum and denounce all those who participated in it. Some communist and socialist members of parties however decided to form a new party—the Party for Democracy (PPD)—which allowed them to stand for office. Second, the political party law required that parties that wish to be legalized must acquire a certain number of signatures within a strict time frame. This became problematic because all signatures had to be accompanied by addresses that became public information; thus the threat of government harassment hung over the signature gathering. Third, parties could not accept money from foreign sources: this cut out, for example, contributions from the European Christian Democrats or German stiftungs. Fourth, the government's voter registration law made it difficult for poor people to register; nevertheless 3,300,000 people, about half of the electorate, had been registered by the end of 1987 (Oppenheim 1993, 190–1).

The united campaign against the referendum took the name *Concertació por el No* in early 1988. On August 30 the military junta announced Pinochet to be its candidate for president and set the date for the vote to be held on October 5. Though the opposition had only just over a month to campaign against the referendum, it did have the opportunity to run TV advertisements that proved to be very effective (Quilter 1989). They were also able to place their own election monitors in every precinct while U.S. National Endowment for Democracy money funded a computer system that helped tabulate the returns (Oppenheim 1993, 191–2). In the end, the "No" campaign won 54.7 percent of the vote while the Pinochet regime's "Yes" campaign won 43.0 percent.[20]

Summary

The use of the referendum device in France and Chile from World War II to the present has several significant parallels that may demonstrate common themes in referendum politics in general. The primary theme in both countries was the presidential, or executive, desire for more power. The major actors in referendum campaigns included the executive, the people, the military, and the legislature. Referendum campaigns have demonstrated disparities in opinion between the people and Parliament (1958 and October 1962 in France), between the people and the military (1961 and April 1962 in France), between the executive and the legislature (1958, 1961, October 1962, and 1969 in France), between the executive and the people (1969 in France; 1988 in Chile), and between the executive and the military (1961 and April 1962 in France; 1973 and 1988 in Chile). The executive has miscalculated the response of the people (1969 in France; 1988 in Chile) and the response of the military (1988 in Chile).

Four general points about referendum politics can be made from our discussion of French and Chilean referendum politics. First, executives use *constitutional* referendums to increase their power versus others. Second, the people's position on issues is often closer to the position of the executive than to the position of those groups competing with the executive. Third, the other groups competing with executives for power are usually legislatures but may also be the military. Fourth, executives sometimes misperceive their popularity and ability to win a vote and subsequently lose a referendum campaign.

Thus this set of French and Chilean referendums demonstrates a generalized, typical pattern of referendum politics that can be used in the analysis of other, more complicated referendum cases. Chapters 3 and 4 introduce the referendums of the Soviet and Post-Soviet period and expand upon the base of knowledge presented here in chapter 2. The Soviet and Post-Soviet referendums will not only follow the same patterns of referendum politics established in this chapter but will also expand upon our arguments about referendum politics in transitions.

CHAPTER 3

The USSR Referendum and Republic Counter-Referendums

Referendum cases in the Soviet Union in 1991 demonstrate how the referendum device played a role in elite bargaining not only between executives and legislatures but also between institutions of different federal and regional structures. These cases demonstrate how referendums provide popular legitimacy to govern outside of Soviet Communism and change the distribution of power between federal and regional structures by granting autonomy to the Soviet Republics. Mikhail Gorbachev, the former general secretary of the Communist Party and president of the Soviet Union, introduced the referendum device into the Soviet context in order to outflank political opponents, with various goals, who opposed his goal of maintaining the federal structure of the Soviet Union. This referendum served as the impetus for a slate of votes—counter-referendums—by republics seeking some degree of independence.

The use of the referendum by Mikhail Gorbachev and Boris Yeltsin has widely affected the way in which this device has been used in the Post-Soviet states after Communism. The USSR March 1991 referendum by Gorbachev in particular set a precedent for future leaders because it was the first of its kind in the Soviet Union, though not in all the states it comprised.[1] Gorbachev demonstrated that a leader empowered to propose and/or use this device could employ it against his political enemies and against a lower body of government in a federal structure. The USSR March 1991 referendum set off a rash of counter-referendums by the republics and gave Yeltsin his first impetus to use the device in establishing the Russian presidency. In April 1993 Yeltsin demonstrated how the device could be used against and by one's political enemies in another government body, which in this case was the legislature. Given the high profile these votes commanded, its utility to other actors in the Post-Soviet states became obvious: when one is blocked by another leader or institution from deciding an issue as preferred, one may make an appeal to the people in order to force the decision to be made as one would like. All one needs to do is to be able to write the referendum question, campaign for it for several months, and interpret its results as one would like.

The USSR March 1991 referendum and republic counter-referendums fit the model of referendum politics established by the French and Algerian referendums discussed in chapter 2. These referendums were an attempt to increase the power of executives, or other groups, versus their opponents. These referendum proponents could make use of these referendums because their policy positions were closer to the people than their opponents. These votes, however, introduce a new aspect to referendum politics: referendums being initiated from geographic subunits of a country and sometimes being used to counter, or "duel," national referendum campaigns. These referendums often deal with autonomy issues and may be ethnically driven. Similar to *constitutional* referendums, *autonomy* referendums may also be used to increase the power of the referendum proponent. Referendums on a subregional level, and *autonomy* referendums in particular, tend to weaken national executives at the expense of subregional institutional structures. This makes it hard for a national executive to implement the result of his own referendum even if he wins. Subregional concerns are usually quite different from that of a national executive; therefore these referendums can be politically difficult and devastating for a national executive.

These votes provoke several additional questions: Why did they fail to resolve the issues they were called to address? How exactly would one define a successful referendum result? Successful referendums confer a legitimacy that is recognized not only by the referendum proponents but also by the referendum opponents, along with the elites and masses. Referendums usually grant legitimacy either to a policy or an institution, but they may also be used to confer legitimacy to an individual leader or set of leaders. When referendums yield ambiguous results, however, a vote may not have the desired effect. Ambiguous results may be amplified if personalities and/or highly partisan politics are involved. Ambiguous results may involve a majority of those voting if less than 50 percent of the electorate is represented. Votes may be complicated by differences in national versus regional vote outcomes: for example, certain regions may reject a vote while it passes overall. Also, polarized voting differences between majority and minority citizen groups where a majority wins may mask the resolute opposition of a minority group on an issue. Referendums sometimes may not be able to resolve issues with ambiguous results.

The March 1991 USSR referendum on maintaining the union had an ambiguous result that challenges the determination of whether it was successful or whether it failed. Mikhail Gorbachev called this executive-sponsored referendum as a somewhat last-ditch effort in an attempt to keep the union together. The referendum was one of Gorbachev's options against the factions he was aligned against. Gorbachev, the centrist reformers, the conservatives—represented by Yegor Ligachev—and a majority of the Soviet people *taken as a whole* wanted the union to remain intact while possibly allowing the republics varying degrees of greater independence (Kaplan and Brady 1997). The Democratic Platform—represented by Boris Yeltsin—advocated a truer form of independence from the federal center. Moreover, the Soviet people within certain republics preferred full independence; thus, the position of the people was more ambiguous if one considered the wishes of republic populations on their own.

The referendum was only one of several options that Gorbachev could have used to resolve the issue of the union treaty. He could have allowed each republic to decide its status as per the Soviet Constitution that allowed for secession, brokered a compromise with the republics, let the Politburo or Supreme Soviet decide the matter, or ordered a crackdown on the separatist movements. Instead Gorbachev chose to use the referendum device most likely because of his desire to get the people involved and his expectation that he would win.

Gorbachev's Political Philosophy and the Origin of the Referendum Idea

When Mikhail Sergeyevich Gorbachev used the referendum device in 1991, he may not have known how it was going to affect the political process he had been attempting to control less and less successfully since the advent of glasnost in 1986 and the creation of radical and conservative camps in 1989–1990 in the Communist Party of the Soviet Union (CPSU). Even though there had been some polling done on how the public felt on the issue of re-legitimizing a modified union of Soviet republics, it is very unlikely that Gorbachev either had the predilection or the desire to use poll results to justify him taking a gamble on a vote by the people. In times of stability, it is not hard to accept that a *rational actor* would call a referendum when he or she had a strong belief that the people would support his measure. Often such beliefs are based upon polling results. In Gorbachev's case it is not at all clear he had such a belief based upon polling information; he honestly assumed that a majority of the Soviet people wanted to keep the union together: "I was becoming increasingly aware that the political struggle in the forthcoming period would evolve primarily around the issue of the fate of the Union: to be or not to be—and if it were 'to be,' what shape would it take? In the final analysis, the success or failure of economic, political and legal reforms also hinged on answers to these questions. I believed that none of these problems could be resolved without the participation of our people. I was honestly convinced that, on the whole, they would favour the preservation of the Union and its transformation into a full-fledged federation" (Gorbachev 1996, 584). Gorbachev had strong prior beliefs that the people would support a vote on the Union Treaty, and, therefore, had no need of polling results. In short, he thought he knew the answer.

Gorbachev believed that the "people" were closer to his view on the Union Treaty than that of the CPSU, and he wanted to use the people to overcome some of the CPSU views. However, Gorbachev did not realize that though the "people" might be on his *side*, they might also be farther Left than he on the policy space on republic independence. In other words, the "people" were slightly more radical than Gorbachev was on the subject. Even though the median voter of the electorate might want greater sovereignty and power for the republics, the median voter was probably still against giving any republic its independence.[2]

The fact that he wanted the people to express their opinion through a referendum, though, was a revolutionary act; nevertheless it should not be viewed as entirely unexpected. Gorbachev had the capability to transcend Soviet tradition and doctrine because he believed in the social democratic aspects of Marxism–Leninism. Two of the strongest tenets of Gorbachev's political philosophy had to do with the "rule of law" and "energizing the mass of the people" (Walker 1991). This is not to suggest that he did not also see the Communist Party as the ruling entity of the Soviet Union for he most assuredly did.

On the contrary, his goal until late in his tenure as general secretary of the Communist Party was to make the Party more responsive to the people and give them a real, democratic role in its decision-making as the rhetoric of the early Communists, particularly Lenin, had stated. He was a true democratic socialist from the beginning. He believed that the country had begun to rot politically and stagnate precisely because the people had no role in decision-making. Though Stalin took it to an extreme, decision-making in the Soviet Union was highly centralized under General Secretaries Khrushchev and Brezhnev; this tactic served primarily as a means to consolidate power by the general secretary (Breslauer 1982). Gorbachev attempted in successive piecemeal attempts to involve more people in the soviets and various other institutions beginning with his efforts in the countrywide policies of glasnost.

It is noteworthy that the referendum device combines the ideas of the "rule of law" and "energizing the mass of the people" into one institution. The referendum device makes law by allowing the people to vote public measures or actual statutes up or down. In fact, no other democratic institution allows the people such direct control in law making. Therefore it should be no surprise that Gorbachev utilized the device even though it had never been used before in the entire history of the Soviet Union or, for that matter, the Russian state. Nor should it be a surprise that he used it for his own political purposes, for better or worse, in the name of the people.

Gorbachev's Views on the Role of the People in the Political Process

Gorbachev was a socialist who believed that democratic ideas are at the center of socialism. Therefore, one of Gorbachev's fundamental goals was to make the Soviet Union more democratic, but not necessarily along the lines that the Western concept of democracy dictates. In the West, democracy meant that the people have supreme power, that people rule directly or indirectly through elected representatives, and that decision-making was based upon majority rule. The more democratic Soviet state Gorbachev attempted to fashion would have been distinct from other democratic states if for no other reason than the continued leading role of the Communist Party. Nevertheless, Gorbachev's ideas about "putting the people at the center of the state" began to create a unique political environment from which the referendum device sprang.

Gorbachev wrote that in order to reform the country into a higher form of socialism, the unrealized potential of the people must be tapped and used. He quoted Lenin as saying that socialism and democracy cannot be separated; socialism has the interests of the people as its goal (Gorbachev 1988, 18). It attempts to bring the masses to power and therefore democratic ideas must be instituted. Socialism has no ready-made stages of development; it must be created as we go along with the people serving as the ultimate judge of the socialist system since they have the power to accept or reject it. Therefore the input of the people is absolutely essential and necessary to reform the country (Gorbachev 1988, 18–19). Restructuring, he said, is a great task that can only be accomplished by a great effort and the people need to be "woken up." The individual must be involved in all processes because only people can make history (Gorbachev 1988, 15).

The people, he has written, will build a society that is politically and socially active, spiritually rich, fair, and thoughtful. The people can only do this, though, if they are first uplifted themselves. Gorbachev believed that the people should be respected in all matters of restructuring and work in order to give them moral strength. Everyone must feel like their efforts are worthwhile and that they are trusted. Only in this way will a strengthened people be able to reform society (Gorbachev 1988, 16).

This component of "activating the human factor" had many important tasks in Gorbachev's rhetoric. First, Gorbachev wanted to mobilize the people to help reform the country. Second, he attempted to make the Party and the state legitimate in the eyes of the masses by addressing their concerns and including them in the process. Third, in order to carry out great change, he believed that the people needed to be convinced of its need and give their own input in order for reform to be relevant and powerful.

The quantity and quality of political participation by the Soviet people under Gorbachev, though, did not equate to majoritarian rule. Political participation in the Soviet Union, as in every society, is usually the product of its political culture, but for most of the history of the USSR participation had been regimented by the Communist Party. Citizens were drawn into the implementation of policy but not into its formation, and there was usually no room for competition and electoral choice: Soviet elections have had only one candidate to select from and the appearance of 99 percent voter turnouts was important to the Party. The Party declared that Soviet society was fundamentally harmonious because it had done away with capitalism and class antagonism. Thus, it was possible for one ruling party to represent the whole of the people— as the Communist Party claimed that it did—and thereby justify a monopoly on political power. So, while involuntary participation was extremely high, voluntary participation and competition in recognized government bodies was extremely low.

Gorbachev helped to increase voluntary participation and competition through political reforms and indirectly by allowing "informal groups" to flourish. The first significant actions were the glasnost policies he initiated in 1986. These improved the relationship between the intelligentsia and the political leadership through a loosening of restrictions on public discussion (Lampert 1990, 129). From 1987 onwards, the political system itself began to be reformed to allow for greater public participation (Lampert 1990, 129). A degree of political choice and accountability was introduced through multi-candidate elections and the establishment of a sitting parliament—the Supreme Soviet. The strong emphasis on legal guarantees suggested greater rights for individuals and groups that would make the democratization process more difficult to reverse.

The most important development at the time, however, was the forementioned *informal groups* that were independent of the Party and state bodies. These groups, all initiated by the people, focused around a wide range of issues from leisure clubs with no political focus to Popular Fronts with substantial political platforms. *Informal groups* were extremely significant because they represented a break with tradition; in the past the Soviet leadership was afraid of such social spontaneity. They consisted mostly of young people, though in the political groups anyone less than 40 years old was considered "young." The membership in these political groups in particular accounted for approximately 10 percent of all the individuals in February 1988 who belonged to organizations (Lampert 1990, 131). These political groups covered the entire spectrum of ideologies and multiplied rapidly in 1987–1988 after initially crystallizing around the intelligentsia in Moscow and Leningrad. Certain issues, like the environment, inspired broad-based support both geographically and among different strata of people. Before Gorbachev, such activity had been inconceivable.

Gorbachev's rhetoric concerning public participation in the political process changed very little over his tenure in office though much had been clarified since his exploration of the topic in his book *Perestroika*. Gorbachev still talked of ". . . political reforms, directed toward people's rule and putting the individual back into the political process."[3] He talked of his success in increasing participation and often described what the political situation was like before his reforms:

> . . . Before, the individual in this country was like a nut or a bolt. I know how nuts and bolts are treated. I was a combine operator for six years. When something breaks down and has to be repaired, you go look in a box where nuts and bolts are scattered about as if it were a junk heap. That's how it was. That was our former democracy. I don't have to be told

what democracy was before 1985. From the office of first secretary of the territory Party committee, which I occupied for almost nine years, I could make decisions on everything without thinking about whether they were in accord with the law or the Constitution. I make decisions, and that was that. I hope I had a conscience. But what about those who had no conscience? You know what kind of decisions they made.[4]

In fact, the success of these and other reforms allowed the expression of needs and wants by the people that led to the instability characteristic of the Soviet Union in the early 1990s. Key indicators of this instability were ethnic strife, labor unrest, and the secession movements of some republics. The principal driver of these public sentiments, though, was the deterioration of the economy, the perceived disparity between the USSR and the West, and movements toward ethnic solidarity.

In conflict with these sentiments, Gorbachev began to defend the leading role of the Communist Party, the socialist system, and the integrity of the union. After the heckling he received at the May Day Parade in 1990, a law was passed making negative comments about the general secretary illegal. Limits upon the free press were established. Efforts by citizens to push their republics to secede from the union were met by violence in both Lithuania and Georgia. On April 9, 1991 Gorbachev called for banning strikes, demonstrations, and rallies until the end of the year. From an outsider's point of view, it began to seem as if he was interested in citizen participation not simply for its own virtues, but to serve the interests and goals he had defined for it.

Winning the Support and Trust of the People

Gorbachev wrote unabashedly about the problems of the Communist Party internally and its relationship with the average Soviet citizen. The Party apparatus, he wrote, had a fundamental disrespect for the law that manifested itself in, for example, bribery and in some cases criminal acts. Working people saw Party leaders protecting one another, getting rich, and suppressing unwanted criticisms. The Party, from Gorbachev's point of view, deserved to lose the respect of the people.[5]

From Gorbachev's perspective, the Party suffered a crisis of legitimacy among the Soviet citizenry because it had lost its moral authority. It had given approval to the crimes of Stalin and the stagnation under Brezhnev. It claimed to represent the whole of the Soviet people when it obviously did not. Party policies were monolithic and were created with little input from the people, and most Soviet citizens held the Party responsible for the current ˙economic crisis. Gorbachev acted to regain the respect of the people by reforming the Party and the country, and he attempted to give the Party credit for it; the country's reforms, he stated, were being carried out by the Party, "the guarantor of perestroika."[6]

Gorbachev's Views on the Role of Law in Society

It must be significant that Gorbachev studied law when he was at Moscow State University; the only other Soviet leader who did so was Lenin. Gorbachev seemed to have a greater respect for the law than other Soviet leaders. For Gorbachev, the institution of law was necessary for democracy to exist because it was designed to protect society from the abuses of power and to secure the rights and freedoms of individuals and groups. As the country went through greater restructuring, the need to secure those changes into law became greater. He cited the example of how changes after the October Revolution abolishing private ownership of the means of production had to be justified and put into law. Otherwise, he said, "the revolutionary process would have faced chaos and it would have been impossible to consolidate our acquisitions, ensure the normal functioning of the Soviet system of government and establish new principles in public life" (Gorbachev 1988, 91–2).

Gorbachev made a point of noting that the law should be flexible and allow the initiative of citizens to develop. Here was a clear reference to a past problem: laws used to be decreed by a plethora of executives and government bodies covering a myriad of topics. In such an environment, it was impossible to stay current. Implying greater freedoms, Gorbachev stated that everything was allowed that was not strictly prohibited by the law (Gorbachev 1988, 93–4). Moreover, Gorbachev noted that the Supreme Soviet in June 1987 had passed legislation outlining a procedure for citizens to subject important questions of political life to nationwide discussion (Gorbachev 1988, 94). The actual legislation that authorized the USSR March 1991 referendum was passed, at Gorbachev's insistence, by the Congress of People's Deputies in December 1990, just three months before the vote took place.

Though the idea of the referendum was nothing new to the Soviet state, it took a leader with nascent democratic ideas to implement the device. The Petrograd Soviet first mentioned referendums in a decree on November 8, 1917 (Butler and Ranney 1994, 178). The July 6, 1923 Soviet Constitution, article 48 in the 1936 Constitution, and article 108 of the 1977 Constitution all provided for a referendum vote.

Even though there has always been significant discussion in the USSR of the device, the first countrywide vote was not held until March 1991.

In summary, Gorbachev was predisposed to the referendum device for three important reasons. First, he wanted to get the "people" involved in the reform process. Second, he thought that he and the "people" shared the same views on reform. Third, the referendum accorded with his ideas on the rule of law. With this reasoning, Gorbachev utilized the referendum device in 1991.

The March 1991 Referendum in the USSR

Preface: Glasnost and Perestroika ca. 1986–1990

The March 1991 referendum in the USSR had its origins in the effort of certain Soviet republics seeking their independence from the center as Eastern Europe had from the Soviet bloc in 1989–1990. Their reasons were the same. First, the leaderships of both the East European states and the Baltic republics felt as if their respective countries would thrive economically, relative to the rest of the Communist bloc, and that their inclusion into the Communist system in the 1940s had hurt their economic development with regards to the rest of Europe. Second, the leaderships of these states had finally been given the opportunity to express their concerns with the introduction of the glasnost, or openness, policy by Gorbachev in the late 1980s.

Gorbachev's reasons for introducing glasnost, though, had precious little to do with granting independence to Eastern Europe, the Soviet republics, and the nationalities that were spread throughout these regions. It did, however, have everything to do with empowering individual Soviet citizens to recognize their economic and social situations and place pressure upon the Communist Party apparat for political change. In this way, Gorbachev hoped to open a second front in his war against Communist Party conservatives who did not wish to respond to his demand to restructure the economy. They did not wish to change because their livelihoods were invested in the current corrupt and stagnant system. On one level, Gorbachev wanted the same thing that every radical reformer who sought independence wanted—economic prosperity. But they had drastically different methods to achieve this goal. The radical reformers wanted to do so by winning independence from the bulk of the Soviet bureaucratic system—in other words, they wanted to downsize and decentralize the *corporation*. Gorbachev simply wanted to overhaul and replace the management of the system but not to destroy it. While economics was the original goal of both Gorbachev and the radical reformers, it quickly became an issue of power and even identity as the various nationalities began to assert their uniqueness.

Thus the strategic, political situation in 1990–1991 consisted of three groups of actors spread across national-, republic-, and city-level positions throughout the Soviet Union. In 1990, these three groups were well represented by factions in the Communist Party as reflected in their behavior at the 28th Party Congress in July 1990. First, there was the conservative faction led by Yegor Ligachev who fought to maintain the *monopolistic* role of the CPSU in politics, society, and the economy. Second, the radical, or *abolitionist*, faction known as the Democratic Platform fought for the CPSU to relinquish its leading role by dissolving party cells and giving up the party's organizational resources (Breslauer 1989, 336). Boris Yeltsin, by the way, had been the most prominent leader in the latter faction. In the middle were Gorbachev and his reformist allies who were neither "monopolistic" nor "abolitionist" (Breslauer 1989, 336). At different times, Gorbachev sided with either the conservatives or the radicals, and he sometimes made compromises to both at the same time—his staunch centrism has been widely recorded.

The positions of various factions within the Soviet elite and the Soviet public placed along a one-dimensional policy space revealed an opportunity to Gorbachev. The conservative CPSU faction was far to the Right while the Democratic Platform was decidedly non-Communist and Liberal. Gorbachev and the centrist reformers definitely leaned toward Communism along with the median voter of the people. Gorbachev believed that the people were somewhere close to his position. In part this shows why Gorbachev may have decided not to work very closely with the democrats: he probably believed that he could not get the Union Treaty he wanted with them on board because of their strong liberal, pro-independence stand.

Gorbachev clearly did not want to see the break-up of the Soviet Union; nevertheless, he compromised in the end in order to see a weakened union agreed upon in a treaty by a majority of the republics. It was this compromise in the end that sparked the 1991 August Coup attempt by hard-liners in the Soviet government. Before this compromise had been brokered and its consequences played out before the world on television in the fall of 1991, Gorbachev had attempted to use the referendum to decide the matter with relative ease by going around all of the participants in this struggle, the conservatives and radical reformers, by appealing directly to the people for legitimation. In the end, it did not work, but why not? On the surface, tactically, it seemed like the perfect move. But while Gorbachev was a brilliant tactician, his failings throughout his tenure as leader of the Soviet Union can be blamed on his lack of strategic insight (Reddaway 1990, 125–40) and ignorance of how individuals other than himself could possibly have different beliefs, especially beliefs tainted by nationalism (Lapidus 1989, 92–108).

The Union Treaty

The union treaty, first attempted by referendum and then proposed through compromise with republic leaders, was the direct cause of the August Coup attempt (Remnick 1994, 450–2). The coup attempt's failure highlighted the real power held by republic leaders, such as Boris Yeltsin, and the weakness of the hard-liners who attempted to save the federal structure as it was. Such a disparity of real power based ultimately upon popular support, that is legitimacy, made the existence of the Soviet Union a contradictory fact. Gorbachev himself resigned from the Communist Party and eventually was forced to usher out the existence of the USSR and his presidency.

Gorbachev's first suggestion to use a referendum to decide a policy matter came much before his proposed draft union treaty in November 1990. He had earlier suggested a referendum on his May 1990 transition program to a "regulated market economy" (Staff of the Commission on Security and Cooperation in Europe 1991, 1). In October he had suggested a referendum on legalizing private property: he later repeated this proposal several times in his dialogue with the Fourth Congress of People's Deputies in December 1990. Gorbachev had often before used democratic devices as tactical weapons. In 1987, he proposed multi-candidate elections to Communist Party posts in order to subvert apparatchiks who resisted perestroika. Gorbachev attempted to shake up the CPSU as a whole with his proposal to elect a new countrywide Supreme Soviet in late 1988. Over the years, the CPSU as an institution had attempted to thwart his economic and political reforms. Over time these tactics backfired as the impetus for change increasingly originated from below. In July 1989, Union-wide, republic-level Supreme Soviet elections approved by Gorbachev were more of a concession to striking coal miners (Staff of the Commission on Security and Cooperation in Europe 1991, 2). Nevertheless, Gorbachev probably thought that his proposed use of the referendum device in December 1990 was a smart move (Matlock 1995, 476).

By suggesting the union referendum in December, Gorbachev was attempting to out-maneuver three politically powerful and ascendant actors: the Baltic republics and their declarations of independence, the newly elected 1990 republic legislatures and their sovereignty declarations, and Boris Yeltsin as nationalist leader of the Russian republic. The policy positions of Gorbachev, the Baltic republics, and the republics who declared "sovereignty"[7] provide a telling account for the reason that Gorbachev proposed the referendum. Gorbachev's position on a one-dimensional policy space lies solidly on the side of the status quo and a majority of Soviet citizens while the Baltic republics' position definitely favored independence. The Russian republic, like most other republics whose legislatures declared their sovereignty, wanted greater independence from Moscow but not complete independence; therefore, Russia can be placed right in the middle.

Concerns About the Timing, Wording, and Possible Interpretation of the March 1991 Referendum

Gorbachev's November draft union treaty was centralizing and restrictive and not one republic accepted Gorbachev's draft union treaty without some major amendments. All republics wanted a measure of control over their own affairs, especially their natural resources, but Gorbachev was not willing to make the concessions the republics wanted. Instead, he attempted to undercut their authority by appealing directly to the population at large through a referendum. Gorbachev formally proposed the union treaty referendum at the Fourth Congress of People's Deputies on December 17; it was approved by the USSR Supreme Soviet on December 24. On January 16 the USSR Supreme Soviet made the holding of the referendum official by setting the date for March 17 and proclaiming that it was mandatory for all republics and citizens. Its results, according to the resolution, were "binding on the whole territory of the USSR and could be rescinded only by means of a new referendum."[8]

The leaders of the republics had several objections to the union referendum. Leaders of republics seeking independence argued that the referendum was being initiated from the center with no input from the republics in order to sustain the dominance of the federal structure. Leaders of conservative republics not seeking independence felt the vote was unnecessary because support for the federation among their constituents was strong. Moreover they worried that an unnecessary vote would waste time, energy, and money to organize.[9] Nursultan Nazarbaev of Kazakhstan and Saparmurad Niyazov of Turkmenistan both expressed concern about holding a referendum in a time of instability (Sheehy 1991). This latter concern foreshadows how a referendum increases tension between its participants and may possibly lead to conflict.

The referendum also came under attack in Moscow. Observers pointed out that only 26 percent of those on voter lists could decide the issue (50 percent plus one of voters who consisted of at least half of the USSR's eligible voters) whereas the April 1990 law on secession required at least two-thirds of eligible voters in a republic (Sheehy 1991, 6). Referring to the December 27, 1990 law on referendums, jurists questioned the legality of a referendum that attempted to decide an issue that was completely within the competence of an individual republic to decide and therefore posed an inappropriate question for an all-union referendum.[10] Few people understood exactly how the vote would be counted: would the vote in each republic be binding only within it or would the overall vote be binding on individual republics? Gorbachev did make clear that a "No" vote in a republic would not mean its immediate and automatic secession from the Soviet Union.

The wording of the question itself came under heavy fire: "Do you consider necessary the preservation of the Union of Soviet Socialist Republics as a renewed federation of equal sovereign republics, in which the rights and freedoms of an individual of any nationality will be fully guaranteed?" Because the question actually contained several questions, how could one answer it with a simple "Yes" or "No"? How could one "preserve" something that was not yet "renewed"? The question assumed that the union that survived would be "socialist" and not just a unified state. Moreover, one could only vote for an alternative union by voting for the total disintegration of the present one.[11] An affirmative answer could be interpreted to mean anything from support for local soviets as a form of state power to the government's use of harsh measures to resolve interethnic tensions.[12] Moreover, no one really knew what the final clause on "equal rights" meant at all. These criticisms led a group of academics to argue that the wording itself violated the referendum law since it was not "clear and neutral" in meaning. The referendum, they concluded, was "politically undesirable, juridically inaccurate, and sociologically unprofessional" and they urged its cancellation.[13] The central Soviet authorities, however, dismissed these objections.

The Response of the Republics to the All-Union Referendum: Boycotts, Counter-Referendums, and Simply Changing the Question

The model of referendum politics established through case studies of the French Fifth Republic referendums and the Chilean referendums in the 1970s and 1980s becomes more complex with the inclusion of geographic, political subunits of a state into the set of actors involved in referendum politics: executives, legislatures, the people, and the military. Executives, legislatures, and the people must now be distinguished between their federal manifestations and their respective republic-, or substate-, level positions. Thus, one can have a federal, or national, executive like de Gaulle and Gorbachev, or one can have a republic-level leader like Boris Yeltsin of the Russian Soviet republic. Legislatures may now not only take the form of a federal Supreme Soviet or Parliament but may also exist on the republic, or substate, level. Moreover, the people's interest may either be expressed on a federal level or from the perspective of a particular republic unit. In this way, Soviet and Post-Soviet referendum politics differs significantly from the model of referendum politics established from the earlier French and Chilean cases.[14]

When Gorbachev insisted on fighting the battle over the union in the public arena, the republics soon realized that there were several ways to frustrate his plans. The republics learned one tactic of referendum politics quickly: if one does not like the current referendum on the table, boycott or block it. Moreover, they also proposed their own referendums, or counter-referendums. On January 17, the day after the USSR Supreme Soviet set the date of March 17 for the union referendum, Lithuania announced its plans to hold a "public opinion poll" on independence on February 9. The Baltic republics had too much at stake to allow Gorbachev to hold his referendum exactly as planned. Instead, these republics decided to boycott the union referendum and hold their own "public opinion poll" on independence—though in fact it was technically a referendum. Armenia, Moldova, and Georgia also boycotted the referendum but only Georgia among these three also called an independence vote. Russia, Ukraine, Uzbekistan, and Kyrgyzstan officially held Gorbachev's question but decided to add a question to the all-Union ballot to be asked exclusively in their own republic; Ukraine, Uzbekistan, and Kyrgyzstan added a question on their status as an "equal sovereign republic." One republic, Kazakhstan, utilized the subtle tactic of changing the wording of the question. In this way, Kazakhstan made it harder for Gorbachev and easier for itself to interpret the wording of the question. Only Azerbaijan, Belorussia, Tajikistan, and Turkmenistan held the referendum as Gorbachev wanted. In the end, each republic's response seemed to correspond with its internal distribution of power and attitude toward independence.

In the Russian republic, for example, the conflict was not only Center versus periphery but also Gorbachev versus Boris Yeltsin. Yeltsin had been an ally of Gorbachev's in his push to reform until he openly criticized Ligachev, the CPSU's second in command, and Gorbachev himself for the slow pace of reform in a meeting of the Central Committee. In response, Gorbachev publicly chastised and humiliated Yeltsin and removed him as head of the Moscow Communist Party organization on November 11, 1987. But by the spring of 1990, Yeltsin had risen to chairman of the Russian republic's Parliament and was the popularly recognized opposition leader to Gorbachev and the Center.

Yeltsin used the upcoming vote on the union referendum as an opportunity to hold a vote in the Russian republic on establishing the institution of the presidency. For Yeltsin, boycotting the referendum was too strong an action to take at the time, but introducing another question for the Russian people to answer was not. Yeltsin decided to add a question to the Russian republic ballot that would set the groundwork for an institution—a popularly elected Russian presidency—which would allow him to directly challenge the authority and legitimacy of Gorbachev. On January 25, the presidium of the RSFSR Supreme Soviet agreed to hold the all-union referendum and recommended that the Russian Supreme Soviet consider additional questions. Yeltsin was then able to place his question on the ballot: "Do you consider necessary the introduction of the position of President of the RSFSR, elected by universal suffrage?"

In addition, the *domino effect* of referendum begetting referendum continued to the local level where anti-Yeltsin forces and others devised additional questions of their own on regional and city levels. Most of these questions were relatively harmless; nevertheless, the precedent had been set for challenges to the sovereignty of the Russian republic through the referendum device. These challenges would multiply in just a few years.

In Ukraine, the addition of a republic-wide question on its autonomy reflected the alignment of political forces within its Parliament. The Communist Party majority within the Ukrainian Supreme Soviet did not want to add an additional question, but pressure from the democratic opposition Narodna Rada and some moderate communists resulted in a February 13, 1991 decision, by a vote of 287 to 47, to add a specific republic question. This additional question was a compromise fashioned by Presidium Chairman Leonid Kravchuk and it revealed a split between hard-line and moderate Communist Party deputies. On February 27 the Ukrainian Supreme Soviet adopted the text for the question: "Do you agree that Ukraine should be part of a Union of Soviet Sovereign Republics on the basis of the declaration on the state sovereignty of Ukraine?" Note that this question distinguishes itself from the all-union question by only proposing a confederation of sovereign republics as opposed to a "renewed federation."

Similar to Russia, localities within Ukraine also put a separate question on the ballot, but the Center–periphery conflict here was more acute. Deputies from the three western Ukrainian oblasts of Lviv, Ivano-Frankivsk, and Ternopil formulated a third question on Ukraine's independence outside the Union: "Do you agree that Ukraine should be an independent state, which independently decides its domestic and foreign policies, which guarantees the equal rights of all citizens, regardless of nationality and religion?" Western Ukraine, which came under Soviet control only during World War II, was in the forefront of the Ukrainian independence movement. By contrast, Eastern Ukraine was more heavily populated by ethnic Russians who may have given that region less impetus to secede.

Kazakhstan's President Nursultan Nazarbaev ingeniously both complied with Gorbachev's wishes and asserted his republic's autonomy by simply changing the wording of the question. He had argued earlier that the all-union referendum was not needed in republics whose population was not split about inclusion within the Union; he saw the upcoming vote as unnecessary and a waste of resources. Furthermore he argued that the referendum was planned without any input from the republics and represented an attempt by the Center to assert its dominance.[15] Erik Asanbaev, the chairman of the Kazakhstan Supreme Soviet, explained to Pravda on March 15 that the all-Union question had itself raised many questions and seemed "somewhat ponderous and diffuse" to the republic's legislators.

At the February 15 extraordinary session of the Kazakhstan Supreme Soviet, 259 of 286 deputies voted to make it "simpler and more comprehensible," by giving it the following wording: "Do you consider it necessary to maintain the USSR as a Union of sovereign states of equal rights?" It left out the clauses in the all-Union question on "renewing the federation" and the "equality of rights of all peoples." These phrases struck republic leaders as giving Moscow carte blanche authority to apply central military force inside republics where ethnic Russians resided because Moscow had justified such intervention before. The January 1991 crackdown in Lithuania by central military forces killed tens of people and injured more than a hundred in the name of defending ethnic Russians living in Lithuania.

In summary, the republics' responses to Gorbachev's federal referendum highlight several points. First, federal referendums can lead to counter-referendums from substate, or periphery, governments if these governments have an adequate political institutional infrastructure. In these cases, republic-level Supreme Soviets and executives were able to propose and/or call their own referendums in response to the union referendum. Several of the republic-level Supreme Soviets had already been "dueling" with federal institutions and Gorbachev. Though Gorbachev may have been surprised by the use of the referendum device against him, he could not have been surprised about the opposition he encountered from various republics. Second, the nature of substate government responses differs according to their geographic location, history, and economic relationship with the federal center. Table 3.1 shows the tendency of the Baltics to have been the republics most opposed to the all-Union referendum followed by the Caucasus. The Slavic republics' response leans slightly toward opposition while the response of the Central Asian republics is the most favorable to Gorbachev on the whole. The referendum categories presented in table 3.1 actually form a scale of pro-independence vs. pro-union sentiment. The categories proceed from a vote for independence to a boycott of the all-Union referendum to a vote for sovereignty within the USSR structure. The next category—changing the wording of a question—is a more pro-Union than pro-independence maneuver while the last category—holding the question as Gorbachev wished—is strongly pro-Union.

Table 3.1 Republic response to the All-Union referendum by political geographic categories

	Pro-independence < ——————————————— > Pro-Union				
Category	Independence from USSR	Boycotted	Sovereignty within USSR or another question	Changed question	Held as Gorbachev wished
Baltics	Estonia, Latvia, Lithuania	Estonia, Latvia, Lithuania			
Caucasus and Moldova	Georgia	Georgia, Moldova, Armenia			Azerbaijan
Slavic republics			Russia, Ukraine	Kazakhstan	Belorus
Central Asian			Kyrgyzstan, Uzbekistan		Tajikistan, Turkmenistan

Interpreting the Results of the March 1991 Referendum: Success or Failure?

The all-Union referendum on the union treaty had four significant effects upon Soviet politics in 1991. First, it focused the attention of the entire USSR for three months on the most divisive issue in the political discourse. Second, Gorbachev's apparent "victory" gave him a measure of over-confidence with regard to his ability to get all sides to agree upon a union treaty. Third, the all-Union referendum provoked independence referendums by many republics and regions that otherwise might never have called a public vote. Fourth, it gave Yeltsin the impetus to institute the Russian presidency through which he eventually challenged Gorbachev's authority. The official results of the March 17 referendum gave Gorbachev an electoral victory; its political efficacy, though, was unknown. Eighty percent of the citizens entitled to vote participated in the referendum; 76.4 percent of this number voted in the affirmative for the union treaty question. Therefore, 61.1 percent of the electorate union-wide supported Gorbachev's call for a renewed union of Soviet socialist republics.[16] Though Gorbachev won the referendum, the vote did not ensure a long-term victory.

The results of the referendum vote on the republic level were mixed at best. Estonia, Latvia, Lithuania, Georgia, Moldova, and Armenia all officially boycotted the referendum. Republics that had officially boycotted the vote still had citizens who participated after being organized; for example, in Lithuania, citizens voted in local soviets, enterprises, and military units. None of the results from these elections should be trusted, however: numerous and serious voting irregularities were cited with typical cases including nonresidents voting and individuals voting multiple times.

Several republics that decided officially to participate supplemented the ballot with additional questions that disallowed any straightforward analysis of the all-Union question. In the Ukraine, for example, 70.16 percent voted "yes" on the all-Union question, but 80.17 percent also voted "yes" on the republic question asserting Ukrainian sovereignty. The best interpretation of this seems to be that while Ukrainians supported a renewed Soviet Union, their affirmative response to the republic question suggested that the type of union they desired was closest to a confederation or commonwealth of states. Similar sovereignty votes were also held in Kirghizia and Uzbekistan. In Kirghizia, 94 percent voted "yes" on the all-Union question while 62 percent voted "yes" on Kyrgyz sovereignty. In Uzbekistan, 93.7 percent voted "yes" on the all-Union question while 93.9 percent voted "yes" on Uzbek sovereignty. The Russian republic, instead of holding a vote on its sovereignty, voted on an additional question that addressed establishing the office of president by universal suffrage—a vote that had a powerful, long-term effect. Russians voted 69.9 percent in favor of establishing the Russian presidency while voting 73 percent in favor of the all-Union question.[17] Kazakhstan did not include any additional questions on the ballot; instead, the republic's leaders, as stated above, craftfully changed the wording of the question. The modified question, which still called for "maintain[ing] the USSR as a Union of sovereign states," passed with 94.1 percent of the vote.

Only Belorussia, Azerbaijan, Tajikistan, and Turkmenistan conducted the vote as Gorbachev wanted; they voted 83, 92, 96, and 97.7 percent in favor of the all-Union referendum. However, voting irregularities and violations have been cited in each of the republics except Turkmenistan. The suggestion, though, that essentially everyone who voted in Turkmenistan also voted in favor of the all-Union referendum—official reports declare that there was a 97.7 percent turnout with all 97.7 percent voting "yes"—serves as the best evidence that the vote in Turkmenistan was rigged (Davydov 1991).

Moreover, no one actually understood what the mandate of an affirmative vote dictated (Matlock 1995, 478). Would it allow Gorbachev to put more pressure on the republics to sign his draft union treaty and/or would it grant Gorbachev a measure of popular legitimacy—a legitimacy he did not possess since he had never put himself up for election before the Soviet populace? In both the domestic and foreign-policy realms, Gorbachev's popularity was in decline. The referendum in the end did not seem to affect either his ability to place pressure on the republics to sign the treaty as it then stood or boost his popularity. The CPSU and the USSR Supreme Soviet clearly seemed ready to interpret the vote as a popular mandate and poised itself to force the republics to ratify the soon to be completed union treaty and new USSR Constitution. The Politburo saw the vote as a mandate to "act resolutely and consistently," and "by lawful means to strengthen order, tighten discipline . . . and stabilize the situation."[18]

The March 17 Russian referendum's mandate to create the presidency, on the other hand, was very clear. The Russian referendum established the position of president of the Russian Soviet Federative Socialist Republic with the approval of 69.9 percent of the Russians voting. On June 12, Boris Yeltsin won the first popular election for president with 57.30 percent of the vote in a field of six candidates.[19] It was a considerable defeat for the Communist Party; the CPSU commented afterwards that its leaders had "finally lost authority" (Center for the Preservation of Contemporary Documentation 1991).

The Union Treaty and Elite Conflict after the March 1991 Referendum

What the referendum did do was increase the tension in society between its constituent parts. As the Staff of the Commission on Security and Cooperation in Europe reports, "It laid bare the conflicts between center and republics, between republics and their constituent parts, between different nationalities inhabiting those regions and between political movements already inclined to view their differences in Manichean terms" (Staff of the Commission on Security and Cooperation in Europe 1991). The vote made clear the waning support among the republics for the union, especially the close vote in the Ukraine (Matlock 1995, 494). The March 1991 referendum spawned independence referendums in Lithuania, Latvia, Estonia, the western region of the Ukraine, Armenia, and Georgia. On the other hand, the affirmative vote in the referendum gave Gorbachev, the CPSU, and the USSR Supreme Soviet a degree of popular legitimacy to maintain the cohesiveness and strength of the union and directly challenge republics' independence movements. In this way, instead of solving the union treaty issue, it created a stalemate between the center and republics and hardened pro-Union Communist hard-liners and pro-independence republic secessionists.

The stage for future conflict had been set. The hard-liners, having "won" the referendum vote and therefore legitimacy to fight for the maintenance of the USSR, now simply perceived the breakaway republic leaders as the enemy and were emboldened to "save" the union. Gorbachev, who had come under increasing pressure from hard-liners and criticism from democratic forces for siding with the conservatives, decided to make another strategic shift: this time away from the hard-liners and toward his former democratic allies. In making this shift, once again Gorbachev wanted to portray himself as the reasonable man who occupied the Center of the political spectrum. He reached out to and won the temporary support of Yeltsin and held an impromptu "summit" with the leaders of the nine republics who seemed willing to stay inside some type of confederation.[20] On that very day, the far Right in the Communist Party had convened a meeting of the Central Committee with the goal of ousting Gorbachev, but they had no success. It did serve, though, as a wake-up call to the democratic opposition that there was still a genuine threat to the Right of Gorbachev in the political spectrum (Gwertzman and Kaufman 1992).

Nevertheless, as Gorbachev came closer to a compromise with the republic leaders on a union treaty, hard-liners became more determined to oust him and return the country to the Soviet rule of the bad old days. The treaty that Gorbachev was prepared to sign on August 20 gave significant power and autonomy to the republics and easily allowed the Baltics to gain their independence. Gorbachev had been warned by American officials, Boris Yeltsin, and other democratically inclined politicians that a coup attempt was near; he had even been told the identity of the plotters (Remnick 1994, Part IV). Gorbachev could neither be convinced of the imminent threat of a coup nor did he perceive the many clues leading up to it. Two days before he was to sign the union treaty in Moscow, he was paid an unexpected visit at his Crimean vacation home by a delegation from the State Committee for the State of Emergency. Members of the delegation included a Politburo member, an army general, a representative from the military-industrial complex, his personal assistant, and the head of the KGB's Ninth Directorate, which was charged with the protection of the Soviet leadership. They gave Gorbachev the option of joining them or resigning and informed him that no union treaty would be signed on August 20 (Remnick 1994, 455).

Ultimately, the State Committee for the State of Emergency failed to sustain the coup because of their incompetence and the resistance provided by many citizens, particularly Boris Yeltsin. The coup plotters did not have a clear vision of what to do after calling a state of emergency, and many began to fall into a stupor, sometimes alcohol induced. Though they had ordered military forces to enter Moscow, they were not prepared to use them against the citizenry or other politicians. Many Soviet citizens resisted the brandishing of military arms by querying the soldiers as to what they were doing, and asking them to simply go home (Remnick 1994, 466). The soldiers for their part were not prepared to fire upon their own people. Boris Yeltsin played the most significant role by projecting himself as the leader of the resistance and rallying the people around him: most memorably when he stood upon a Soviet T-72 tank in front of the Russian Parliament building and addressed the citizenry with a bullhorn. As the coup collapsed in the next few days, Boris Yeltsin emerged as the Soviet politician with the most legitimacy supplanting Gorbachev's leadership role of the Russian people.

Summary

Gorbachev's attempt to mobilize popular support backfired because he considered only the position of the typical, or *median voter*, in the USSR. He failed to consider the variability of opinion in the republics, the powerful role that nationalism was beginning to play, and the possibility that the referendum could become a tool for the republics to legitimize their own political positions. This was not a problem for de Gaulle given the long tradition of unitary government in France. Nor was it a problem for Pinochet in the autocratic structure he had created. But it was a problem for Gorbachev given the vociferous Supreme Soviets in the republics that had been created by his previous reforms.

CHAPTER 4

Bargaining and Power in Russian Referendums

Though referendums clearly grant popular legitimacy, it is not always clear what the effects of referendums will be in highly contested political debates. The 1991 Soviet referendum, designed to settle the issue of the union, instead led to numerous independence referendums. The referendums in Russia in 1993 also had widely varying effects: the April 1993 referendums failed to resolve conflict over policy in April 1993 between the executive and legislature but the December 1993 referendum legitimized a strong presidential system with a vote on a new Russian constitution. Even though the Congress of People's Deputies chairman, Ruslan Khasbulatov, opposed him at every turn, and in most every way, Boris Yeltsin, president of Russia, was able to prevail through their elite battle because of the legitimacy the referendum device bestowed upon him.

The addition of the question on whether to establish the Russian presidency in the March 1991 Russian Soviet republic referendums may have been the single most important act in Soviet and Russian politics since the introduction of glasnost and its quickening by the Chernobyl nuclear disaster in 1986. It was the legitimacy of the popularly elected Russian presidency that gave Yeltsin the authority to challenge the August 1991 Coup plotters. The Russian presidency has also been the only major institution to survive since the break-up of the USSR, having bested the old Congress of People's Deputies in October 1993. It has essentially been the only continuous, institutional link to survive the transition period between the old Communist regime and the nascent democratic one. If Gorbachev had not introduced the referendum device, it is probable that Yeltsin would have introduced the Russian presidency but perhaps not by popular vote and perhaps not in time for the August 1991 Coup attempt.

There had been a shift in the distribution of power between institutions and elites in the Soviet Union, and it had happened as the result of a referendum. Yeltsin's use of the referendum to establish the institution of the Russian presidency gave him an unprecedented platform—in June 1991 he became the first popularly elected leader of Russia, ever. The legitimacy of the general secretary, the Politburo, and the Central Committee of the Communist Party of the Soviet Union paled in comparison. Moreover, the authority that these institutions claimed as being the vanguard of Communist ideology eroded over time as their mismanagement of the Soviet economy and nationalities issues became evident. Thus, the referendum device played an important role in the transition from Communist to democratic rule by conferring legitimacy where none was before.

Conflicts in Russia and the Soviet Union that pitted the president versus legislatures and the federal governments versus substate governments were elite conflicts over the distribution of power. Elites often sought to consolidate more power into their respective institutions in order to implement their goals over the objections of their opponents. The chief example of this was the creation of the Russian presidency in 1991 by Yeltsin in order to have a platform from which to challenge Gorbachev. Elites also called referendums directly on the topic they wished decided in their favor in the hope of getting around their opponents. Gorbachev's referendum on the union treaty was aimed to get around recalcitrant republics. Elite goals that changed the distribution of power between nascent political institutions often had long-lasting effects upon the form of government a newly democratic state established. Thus Russia has developed a strong presidential government as a result of Yeltsin's battles with his opponents. In these conflicts, Yeltsin's use of the referendum device has been central. Even though Gorbachev failed to keep the Soviet Union intact, he did attempt to use a referendum to legitimize a new union treaty among rebellious republics. Therefore elite conflict over power has had a strong influence on the character of political institutions and the distribution of power in them.

Referendums have been used by executives and regional governments to increase their power, but, in doing so, elite-sponsored referendums that change the distribution of power in favor of a referendum actor have also increased tensions between referendum participants. For example, the March 1991 union treaty referendum and the republic autonomy referendums spawned increased tensions between its referendum participants (Staff of the Commission on Security and Cooperation in Europe 1991; see chapter 2 of this study). All of the participants gained confidence coming out of the referendum voting: the hard-liners felt they had won the union treaty referendum, the republics felt as if their autonomy referendums had given them more freedom, and Gorbachev felt confident to pursue ratification of a new treaty having won on the question he called. In fact, Nursultan Nazarbayev of Kazakhstan had warned that a referendum could cause further confrontation between the republics and the center.[1] Likewise, the April 1993 Russian referendums and Yeltsin's dispute with the Parliament in 1992–1993 had Muscovites wondering which side the armed forces might take in a civil war (Remnick 1997, 49–50). These referendums raised expectations and created a situation in which there would be definite winners and losers and created a situation that can best be described as zero-sum.

Changing the distribution of power between elites and institutions in a transition period raises the specter of conflict. High expectations of success and misperceptions of one's opponent's likely actions are usually the precursors to wars between states (Blainey 1973). Likewise, misperceptions among domestic elites in competition over the distribution of power between nascent political institutions in transition suggest a very similar outcome. The April 1993 Russian referendums illustrate the strategic choices that domestic political actors face and how conflict might arise from elites pursuing their goals. Though referendums are not the source of the conflict, they may exacerbate a situation and make conflict more likely.

Pre-Referendum Elite Bargaining in Russia, 1992–1996

The subjects of the political debates by elites from 1992–1996 in the Post-Soviet states can be reduced to two issues: economic liberalization and the continued role of Communism, the Party, and its elites (McFaul 1997). Economic liberalization here is also meant to encompass privatization of state resources. The debate concerning the continued role of Communism was most pronounced in the campaigns for elected office. Communist candidates would often attempt to empathize with the citizenry hardest hit by economic liberalization by promoting socialist economic programs and a slowing of reform. Reform candidates would attack their Communist opponents for being associated with the Soviet Communists responsible for authoritarian regimes, the mass repression of people and ideas, and economic stagnation. Reform candidates themselves would differ on how fast and how far economic liberalization plans should go; nevertheless, they always stood apart from and against the Communists no matter how fractured their ranks became.

Figure 4.1 illustrates the positions of several important actors, groups, and institutions. The spatial model has as its x-, or horizontal, axis the issue of the continued role of Communism with the right-hand side denoting increasing sympathy and identification with Communism and the left-hand side denoting increasing antagonism. The y-, or vertical, axis measures one's position on economic liberalization. Ascending the axis denotes increasing favorability toward economic liberalization. Descending the vertical axis denotes increasing distaste for economic liberalization. In general, attitudes toward Communism are negatively correlated with attitudes toward economic liberalization: increasing favorability toward Communism corresponds with decreasing favorability toward economic liberalization. Thus, the Russian electorate occupies a diagonal, elongated oval space stretching from the upper left-hand

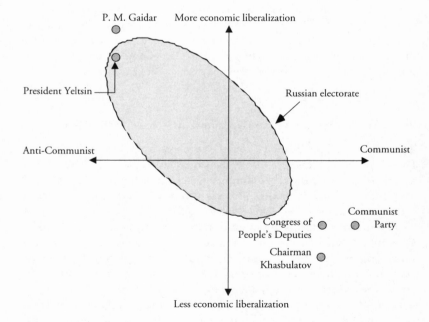

Figure 4.1 Spatial model of elite political debates in russia, 1992–1996

quadrant to the lower right-hand quadrant. This space illustrates how a majority of the Russian electorate had relatively favorable views toward economic liberalization along with relatively negative views of Communism. Former prime minister Gaidar is positioned in the far upper left-hand corner to denote his dedication to aggressive economic reforms and severe anti-Communism. President Boris Yeltsin is positioned beneath Gaidar denoting Yeltsin's equal distaste for Communism but somewhat less enthusiastic but strong support of economic liberalization. On the opposite end of the spectrum, beyond most of the Russian electorate's views, one finds the old Congress of People's Deputies in a position that denotes its distaste for economic liberalization and favorable inclination toward Communism. The Communist Party, though equally disliking economic liberalization, is naturally even better disposed than the Congress to Communism's role in society. Former Congress chairman Khasbulatov, while equal with the Congress' position on Communism, is more adamantly against economic liberalization.

Bargaining between competing sets of elites—economic liberalizers vs. non/slow-liberalizers or Communists vs. anti-Communists—often resulted in policy deadlock because these battles were played out in weak institutions. These institutions were weak because the initial constitutions that set up these systems of government were often compromises between the same competing sets of elites (Walker 1993). These institutions were holdovers from the preceding Communist era that simply did not work well in a democratic Russia. In order to keep one institution or set of elites from dominating the political debate, institutions were given the ability to make laws and to check the law-making or implementation ability of another, but within a system of government no clear rules were established stating how opposing laws or policy debates might be convincingly resolved. The Constitutional Court was given the ability to review the legality of laws, decrees, and electoral issues, but its place in the Russian government's power structure has not been defined. Moreover, as often as it has made a legitimate impact, the Constitutional Court has also been seen as a tool of the executive or legislature (McFaul 1993).

Because of this institutional weakness during transitions, elite usage of the referendum device has a greater impact on the institutional distribution of power than in times of stability. In times of stability, the referendum is used to legitimate policies by elites, but it is not usually used to resolve policy deadlock between institutions because political institutions are usually strong and therefore effective within a system of checks and balances that works decisively to resolve elite disputes. Institutions are formed and reformed usually in transition periods. These transitions may be from authoritarianism or Communism, or follow traumatic international events—like wars—that become the catalyst for change in the political system. An example of a referendum being used after a transition period following a war is the establishment and character of the French Fifth Republic by referendum after World War II. Even though it was more than ten years since the end of World War II, de Gaulle and others placed much of the blame for France's ineptitude before World War II on its parliamentarian government. Therefore, French postwar politics played a decisive role in the adoption by referendum in 1958 of a new constitution. In general, elites have relied upon the referendum device, irrespective of the character of the times, as a way to succeed in fulfilling their goals when blocked by the legislature or the courts.[2]

The legitimacy conferred by a referendum to policies may also be granted indirectly to leaders and institutions representing the policy position because of the explicit linkage between them. Leaders may also link their legitimacy to that of a referendum subject in an attempt to influence a vote beyond the merit of the question. The April 1993 Russian referendum asked not only whether people supported the economic policies of Yeltsin, but also if they trusted him. De Gaulle in the series of referendums he sponsored in the 1960s in France explicitly linked his prestige and reputation to every referendum vote to the point that he threatened to resign if a referendum was not decided in his favor.[3] Referendums used in this way become votes of confidence in leaders.

Furthermore, elite ability to manipulate the referendum device to their advantage endears its usage to them. Elites usually have the opportunity to draft the referendum question in hopes of choosing wording that will give them as much of the vote as possible. Elites also attempt to choose the date of the vote in order to increase their vote total or decrease their opponents'; for example, often elites will attempt to schedule a referendum vote to be held the same day as a general election. Finally, after the referendum vote has taken place, elites may interpret the results to their own benefit. Therefore, the referendum is an extremely attractive device to utilize in one's favor and a hated device to have to fend off.

Referendum Elite Bargaining in Russia

In the early stages of the transition from Communism, elite bargaining over policy often led to deadlock. Battles over policy became battles over the distribution of power between institutions as elites attempted to consolidate the necessary power unto their government body to implement their goals irrespective of the opposition. Presidents desired not only to concentrate power unto themselves, but also often aimed to dismantle the legislatures that opposed them. Regions within states not only created and strengthened regional governmental structures but also strived to become independent of the federal government. Both types of situations created a constitutional crisis that threatened the use of violence by military and security forces to resolve the issue. Elites began to utilize the referendum device not only to resolve these disputes in their favor but also to do so without violence.

The threat of violence, nevertheless, played a central role in elite bargaining. Elites worried about which side the military would take if the policy dispute disintegrated into armed conflict (Remnick 1997, 49–50). The last thing a group of elites wanted was to be pounded into submission by their country's military. Losing an armed conflict would allow the victors carte blanche in the revision of the institutions the losing elites represented. Moreover, the losing elites who survived the armed confrontation would be, at the very least, jailed under severe charges such as treason. Elites who believed the military was on their side were more resolute in their position and acted more aggressively in pressing their agendas than the ones who believed the military would not support them in a violent conflict with their opponents. Elites who believed they would not be supported by the military would develop strategies that attempted to avoid violent conflict but still defended their positions.

When elites did not know which side the military would take, uncertainty confused the participants' strategies. Moreover, if some elites misperceived the information on whom the military supported, both players might have acted with confidence. Such situations had a high probability of leading to violence since each expected the other to capitulate but neither did. The Russian April 1993 referendums are an example of this type of misperception. Both President Yeltsin and Parliament leader Khasbulatov believed the military would support them, their institutions, and their referendum positions. Both called on factions within the military to support them against the other. As it turned out, the forces Yeltsin depended upon came through for him in the end and shelled the Parliament into submission.

Nevertheless, the Russian April 1993 referendums show what happens when legislatures decide to fight back. In some cases, legislatures can put up significant opposition to executives during a referendum campaign, and can change the character of the questions and challenge the interpretation of the votes. Often, in these situations, executives need the support of the military in order to overcome relatively strong legislatures.

The April 1993 Referendums in Russia

The August Coup attempt against Gorbachev drained the old Communist system of its last ounce of legitimacy. The coup was thwarted by the truly heroic efforts of the newly elected president of Russia, Boris Yeltsin, who challenged the coup plotters to return Gorbachev and end their unconstitutional act. In the end, enough of the military complied with Yeltsin while not enough complied with the coup plotters, who, after days in the standoff, quickly began to lose enthusiasm for what they had done.

Gorbachev had not realized the degree to which the system he had worked in and for all his life had been wounded. Directly after his return to Moscow, he addressed a session of the Russian Parliament as if nothing had changed. Yeltsin, eager to punish Gorbachev for his dismissal and public humiliation years before, repeatedly embarrassed Gorbachev by cutting him off, taking his papers from him, and stating that his attachment to the old Communist system would have to end since both Communism and the union were dead. That Yeltsin would behave in such a way was not surprising; what was surprising was the fact that he got away with it without question. It was the public demonstration of what most people knew: Communism, in this form and at least for now, was dead. Gorbachev grudgingly presided over the dismantling of the Soviet Union over the next few months until its official termination the night of December 25, 1991.

Yeltsin, on the other hand, was at the top of his power. He appointed Yegor Gaidar as his prime minister who, with Yeltsin's full blessing, began a program of "shock therapy" based loosely on the economic transition program instituted in Poland. The most concrete aspect of this program that affected every Russian was the allowance of prices of goods to float to their natural level. This had the effect of raising the prices on basic foodstuffs to hyper-inflationary levels. For the old, pensioners, and people on wages still fixed, this was a disastrous turn of events.

The Russian Congress of People's Deputies soon began to criticize Gaidar and then Yeltsin for Gaidar's economic policy. Though they initially supported Yeltsin and the economic policies he was about to institute, they soon jumped on the bandwagon that the reforms had been too extreme and too quick in coming. They claimed to speak for the people who were worst hit by these changes.

The Russian Congress of People's Deputies from 1992–1993 is a good example of a *carryover* institution whose representatives, and views, are increasingly remote from a transitioning polity and society. The Congress had been elected under Gorbachev in 1990 and while the members were elected in multi-candidate races, these elections were not multiparty. Most members represented the old Communist Party, large state enterprises, and collectivized agriculture. Though executives can outflank these institutions, *carryover* institutions can present a major obstacle for a reform effort.

The disconnect between the Congress of People's Deputies and President Yeltsin on economic affairs was the beginning of the conflict between Yeltsin and the Congress. The Congress in November 1991 had voted to give Yeltsin extraordinary powers to institute reforms, but by the time the Seventh Congress of People's Deputies had convened in December 1992, it had reconsidered Yeltsin's powers. In 1992 the conflict between Yeltsin and the standing Parliament—the Supreme Soviet—had reached the point where gridlock had taken hold of the policy-making process. To overcome the deadlock caused primarily by disagreement on economic issues, Yeltsin suggested referendums be called on whether Russia should be a presidential republic, whether a Constituent Assembly should adopt a new constitution, and whether land could be bought and sold. The first two referendum suggestions were explicitly meant to dismantle the Congress and replace it with a bicameral system. The Congress, in turn, passed constitutional amendments that curtailed Yeltsin's extra-constitutional powers. Ruslan Khasbulatov, chairman of the Supreme Soviet and the Congress of People's Deputies, made a compromise with Yeltsin to freeze the constitutional amendments in exchange for holding a nationwide referendum scheduled for April 11, 1993.

The use of polls begins to develop as an interesting story in January 1993. A number of polls were taken throughout the spring of 1993, but their results and especially their effects are not well understood, nor is it known if their implementation held any strategic importance for Yeltsin or the Congress. On January 12, the Omsk Soviet Sociological Center held a "snap" poll of Omsk's population that showed support for Yeltsin and the referendum. On February 21, Karelia's Supreme Soviet voted against holding the referendum by citing an opinion poll that said that a majority of those eligible to vote did not want to take part in the referendum because they felt the integrity of the state would be threatened.[4]

The Russian population in early 1993 was polled several times, but the hard data were not consistently made a part of the public record. Based upon one such poll, the Russian Constitutional Reforms Foundation predicted a referendum turnout of 40 percent. Konstantin

Katanyan, the reporter and writer of the March 10 article this report appeared in, said that if the referendum was a failure it could have unpredictable and even extremely negative consequences for the federation. Given that, he said, the pollsters believed that the referendum should not be held.[5] The next day it was reported that a poll suggested the referendum to be "highly doubtful."[6]

While the battle of the polls went on in the background, current events began to overtake these preliminary plebiscites. On March 7, Yeltsin revealed the questions he proposed for the April referendum: should Russia be a presidential republic, should the supreme legislature take the form of a bicameral parliament rather than a congress, should the new constitution be adopted by a constituent assembly instead of the congress, and whether citizens should be able to buy and sell land. A Yeltsin victory on these questions was seen at the time as questionable.[7] The Eighth Extraordinary Congress of People's Deputies, held from March 10–13, reversed its earlier position by calling off the referendum and furthermore stripping Yeltsin of his extraordinary powers.

The stage was now set for a constitutional and political crisis. The deadlock between Yeltsin and the Congress had reached the point at which both sides resorted to shouting and threat making. On March 20 on nationwide television, Yeltsin announced the imposition of a "special regime" permitting him to rule by decree until April 25, when a referendum on a constitution, a vote of confidence in him, and on a law on new parliamentary elections would be held. The Congress appealed Yeltsin's action to the Constitutional Court while some informally called for his resignation. On March 23 the Constitutional Court ruled Yeltsin's decree unconstitutional without ever seeing the text of the document. On March 24, the decree was published by Yeltsin; the hard copy of the document called only for a "vote of confidence," not a referendum—which required Congressional authorization—and omitted any mention of presidential rule, which undercut calls for Yeltsin's ouster. On March 26 the Ninth Congress of People's Deputies began and promptly started to debate Yeltsin's impeachment. In the end, the vote to impeach Yeltsin lost by only 72 votes; Yeltsin had vowed to ignore the vote if it had passed.

The Wording of the April 1993 Russian Referendums

The Congress decided instead to take action believed to be less volatile and indisputably legitimate—it decided to go ahead and call a referendum. The referendum, though, would be one that included questions it had worded with the goal of embarrassing and politically debilitating the president of Russia. On March 29, it decided to try to beat Yeltsin at his own game. It agreed to an April 25 referendum with the following questions: (1) Do you trust the president of the Russian Federation, Boris Nikolaevich Yeltsin? (2) Do you approve the socioeconomic policies implemented by the president of the Russian Federation and the government of the Russian Federation since 1992? (3) Do you consider it essential to hold preterm elections for the presidency of the Russian Federation? (4) Do you consider it essential to hold preterm elections for the People's Deputies of the Russian Federation?

The first three questions were clearly an attempt by the Congress to embarrass and derail Yeltsin; the wording of the referendum questions was adept. Note the use of the word "trust" in the first question. In the second question, Yeltsin's opponents in the Congress hoped to embarrass Yeltsin in two ways. First it was believed that his economic policy was unpopular, but to make sure it was perceived in such a way, they attached the phrase "and the government of the Russian Federation since 1992" as a clear reference and reminder of former prime minister Gaidar's unpopular shock-therapy initiatives. The third question was an obvious attempt to strip Yeltsin of his office halfway into his presidential term. To put to a vote whether preterm elections should also be held for the Congress as the fourth question was a gamble but probably a risk the deputies felt they could take in order to seem fair to the public. Furthermore, the Congress stipulated that approval of the questions required 50 percent of the eligible voters and not just 50 percent of those who voted; this was instituted in order to make it easier for Yeltsin to lose on the questions, especially the first two. If this congressional stipulation was upheld by the courts, then any vote that failed to garner 50 percent of the eligible voters, or electorate, would be technically invalid by law even if a majority of those voting approved it.

Once more, media attention began to focus around polling and the Constitutional Court. On March 30, the day after the April 25 referendum was announced by the Congress, Yeltsin's supporters challenged in the Constitutional Court the stipulation dealing with the percentage of voters needed to pass a piece of legislation. Beginning about two weeks before the vote, a slew of polls and analyses were released. On April 10 Leonid Sedov of the All-Russian Center for the Study of Public Opinion reported that polls "unequivocally" showed that the question on socioeconomic policy would receive a "No," a "No" to early presidential elections, and a "Yes" to early elections of people's deputies. On the question of confidence in Yeltsin, Yeltsin was likely to fall 3–4 percent short of the 50 percent mark of the total number of voters.[8] On April 14, another pollster said that a Yeltsin win was "impossible"; Yuriy Levada, director of the Center for the Study of Public Opinion, said that Yeltsin had the support of a majority of those who will vote, but did not have a majority of all eligible voters.[9] Leonid Sedov once again reported that no radical changes in the polling results had occurred on April 17, a little over a week before the vote.[10] Moscow Ostankino Television First Channel analyzed an opinion poll on April 19 with the following numbers: (1) Do you trust Boris Yeltsin, the president of the Russian Federation? Yes 53 percent, No 30 percent, Difficulty in answering 17 percent; (2) Do you approve of the social and economic policy being carried out by the president and the government of the Russian Federation since 1992? Yes 39 percent, No 38 percent, Difficulty in answering 23 percent; (3) Do you consider it necessary to hold early elections for the president of the Russian Federation? Yes 32 percent, No 53 percent, Difficulty 16 percent; (4) Do you consider it necessary to hold early elections for the people's deputies of the Russian Federation? Yes 63 percent, No 21 percent, Difficulty 16 percent. The confusing wording of question two was assailed while question four was perceived as the lawmakers' own death warrant.[11]

It was clear that the tide began to turn against the Congress just before the vote. Yeltsin and his supporters had campaigned hard for positive results on the referendum. They simplified their stand by broadcasting to the public that they should vote, "Da, Da, Nyet, Da" or "Yes, Yes, No, Yes." At times it was thought that the insistence on a "No" vote for question three might end up confusing the public and so the rallying call was simplified even further to "Da, Da, Da, Da." Furthermore, Yeltsin won a clear victory when on April 21 the Constitutional Court ruled that the Congress had been too stringent; only the last two questions needed to be approved by 50 percent of the electorate. Yeltsin's opponents began to admit that Yeltsin "would win" the referendum: the Socialist Workers' Party of Russia admitted on Thursday, April 22, that President Boris Yeltsin would win the support of the population, but only thanks to a massive brainwashing campaign on the eve of the referendum.[12] The last of the polls showed "No hopes" for the People's Deputies. Less than 15 percent of Russians supported the Congress of People's Deputies which left "no hopes for a political re-animation of this branch of authority," according to an opinion poll in six Russian regions conducted jointly by the Russian "Mneniye" sociological service, the British Gallup poll, and "Saatchi and Saatchi" company.[13]

The Interpretation and Consequences of the April 1993 Russian Referendums

The manipulation of the referendum device does not end with the vote. Referendum results must be interpreted and framed. Usually the referendum winners have the best opportunity to interpret and frame but anyone may do so including the referendum opponents. Common themes broached in a discussion of referendum results focus on whether or not a majority of the votes and/or electorate are represented in a vote tally, whether or not the turnout was adequate, and the exact meaning of a question's text. When referendum opponents have a platform, such as a legislature, from which to compete with referendum proponents on a vote's interpretation, the process of determining the results of a referendum and implementing its mandate become even more difficult.

Boris Yeltsin and his supporters heralded the results of the April referendum as a victory for the Russian president and his policies of reform, but, in actions that spoke as loudly as their words over the next five months, a resolute group of Communists and nationalists did not. On May 5, 1993, the Central Election Committee released the final results of the referendum vote with the following numbers:

> Do you trust the president of the Russian Federation, Boris Nikolaevich Yeltsin? 58.7 percent of those participating voted "Yes."
>
> Do you approve the socioeconomic policies implemented by the president of the Russian Federation and the government of the Russian Federation since 1992? 53 percent of those participating voted "Yes."
>
> Do you consider it essential to hold preterm elections for the presidency of the Russian Federation? 49.5 percent of those participating voted "Yes."
>
> Do you consider it essential to hold preterm elections for the People's Deputies of the Russian Federation? 67.2 percent of those participating voted "Yes."
>
> Overall, 64.5 percent of the Russian electorate took part in the referendum.[14]

From a Western point of view, Yeltsin had good reason to claim victory having a majority of voters support both him and his policies. But the Russian voters before perestroika lived under a system that often produced near-unanimous votes within governing bodies, an effect of the Communist principle of democratic centralism. Therefore, majoritarian rules that require no more than approximately 51 percent of the vote for victory seemed strange to the Russian population, and victories based upon no more than 60 percent of the vote could have been perceived as questionable. Irrespective of how the population at large felt, it soon became clear that Yeltsin's opponents did not respect his victory. Moreover, because the vote to call new elections for the Congress of People's Deputies fell short of the Constitutional Court mandate of 50 percent of the entire Russian electorate, Yeltsin's opponents in the Supreme Soviet remained in power and became even more determined to resist Yeltsin's moves.[15]

Ruslan Khasbulatov, the Supreme Soviet, and other key hard-liners thwarted every attempt by Yeltsin to capitalize on his referendum victory. Khasbulatov blocked Yeltsin's effort to adopt a new constitution by returning to his old argument that the current document should be amended gradually one piece at a time, and he resisted Yeltsin's call for new, multiparty elections for parliament in the fall of 1993. Inevitably, tensions began to rise between the president and parliament (McAuley 1997, 41). Under Khasbulatov's guidance in the summer of 1993, the Supreme Soviet sought to thwart the tight budget restraints and voucher privatization program of the Yeltsin government's economic policy.[16] Moreover Khasbulatov planned to submit constitutional amendments to the Congress of People's Deputies that would remove Yeltsin as head of the Security Council and take away his ability to sign international treaties.[17] It seemed as if Khasbulatov was attempting to bait President Yeltsin into a showdown that Khasbulatov believed he could win:[18]

> The most plausible purpose of this strategy was to provoke Yeltsin into dissolving the parliament . . . this action would result in [the] automatic impeachment of the president. Khasbulatov clearly expected to win this confrontation, believing that the armed forces would not side with Yeltsin, and that in any event, he would hesitate to use them against the parliament. . . . Speaking on September 18, Khasbulatov barely disguised his strategy. He argued that Yeltsin could not continue to be head of state because his judgment was impaired by alcoholism and that he was attempting to impose a "dictatorial, plutocratic regime." He also warned Yeltsin that any attempt to dissolve the parliament would immediately result in his ouster and urged the army to remain loyal to the constitution.[19]

The military, though, sided with Yeltsin in the end as the conflict escalated. Yeltsin on September 21 issued a set of decrees dissolving Parliament and the powers of its deputies, and set a date for multiparty elections to a new legislative body in December. Khasbulatov and

Aleksandr Rutskoi, the renegade former Russian vice president, refused a compromise consisting of holding simultaneous elections for both president and Parliament and instead barricaded themselves along with supporters in the Russian Parliamentary building, called the "White House." This was the same Russian Parliament building that Yeltsin rallied to during the August Coup attempt. At the time, his two staunchest supporters and resisters to the Coup takers were Khasbulatov and Rutskoi, the two men he now faced barricaded in the same building. Having armed themselves and their supporters, Khasbulatov and Rutskoi's forces instigated several clashes that provoked the hand of the Russian military. After Khasbulatov and Rutskoi's forces ransacked the mayor's building and put the Ostankino television broadcasting center under siege, the military not only intervened at Ostankino but also took the battle to the White House in the heart of Moscow. The military bombarded the parliamentary building with artillery and eventually stormed and took it with elite troops.

Afterward, Yeltsin dismantled the old governing system and set up a presidential democracy with a weak parliament and no vice president. Not only did he hold elections for the new legislative bodies in December 1993, he also called a referendum to legitimize passage of a new constitution formally changing the government system. Even though he had centralized a vast degree of power in the executive, he also took care to give himself, the Russian president, the sole and unilateral means to call future referendums.

The December 1993 Russian Referendum on a New Constitution

The Timing of the December 1993 Referendum

Coming directly on the heels of the victorious October conflict with the Parliament, Yeltsin timed the new elections and the December referendum on a new Russian constitution to take advantage of the clear upper hand he held in the post-conflict political environment. He had been ruling by decree since his dissolution of Parliament on September 21, 1993. Because he had won the referendums called in April 1993 he expected to win on the constitutional vote and to have a parliamentary majority to his liking.

Partisanship and a short amount of time marked the referendum campaign. The Central Electoral Commission was only created on September 29, and the specific commission in charge of providing organizational and financial support to the referendum was not formed until November 22. Yeltsin, threatening the political parties standing for election on November 26, stated that criticism of the draft constitution would be penalized by the withdrawal of their free airtime on television. The chairman of the Central Electoral Commission, Nikolai Ryabov, expressed his hope during a television interview that the constitutional referendum would pass. Moreover, it was suggested by First Deputy Prime Minister Shumeiko that the Communist Party and Nikolay Travkin's Democratic Party be banned from participating in the election because of their pronouncements asking the Russian public to vote down the draft constitution (Staff of the Commission on Security and Cooperation in Europe 1994).

The Russian polity, however, had seemingly been turned off by the infighting among the political elite. The Central Election Committee reported that the turnout for the referendum and election was 54 percent—down 10 percent from the 64 percent turnout of the April 1993 referendums.[20] In all, 58.4 percent of those voting supported the adoption of the new constitution by a referendum question that asked simply, "Do you accept the constitution of the Russian Federation?" (Staff of the Commission on Security and Cooperation in Europe 1994). The constitution needed 50 percent of the electorate to participate and 50 percent of those voting in favor of the referendum for the constitution to be adopted.

The Interpretation and Consequences of the December 1993 Russian Referendum

The consequences of the December 1993 referendum were clear: Russia was now a presidential republic. The draft constitution, now essentially the first new constitution for Russia since the 1978 Soviet Brezhnev Constitution, included elements of the French and American constitutions. The president now had the preponderance of the power with the ability to appoint the prime minister; the head of the Central Bank; the justices of Constitutional Court, Supreme Court, and High Court of Arbitration; the General Procurator, and the High Command of the armed forces. The president can also issue decrees, institute a state of emergency, and introduce martial law. As head of state, the president provides direction for both domestic and foreign policies. Directly elected by the electorate to a four-year term, the president cannot serve for more than two consecutive terms of office (Staff of the Commission on Security and Cooperation in Europe 1994).

The new Russian Parliament is substantially weaker than its predecessor and the president. It is a bicameral legislature with a lower chamber entitled the State Duma and a higher chamber called the Federation Council. Though a president cannot dissolve the Federation Council, he or she may dissolve the State Duma and call for new elections if the lower chamber rejects the "prime minister three times, votes no-confidence in the government twice in three months, or votes no-confidence in the government after the prime minister has asked for a vote of confidence" (Staff of the Commission on Security and Cooperation in Europe 1994). The Parliament, on the other hand, cannot easily impeach the president. First, the Duma must form a commission to determine whether or not the Supreme and Constitutional Courts should rule on if the president has committed a "grave" crime or act of treason. Second, the Supreme Court must rule and then the Constitutional Court must agree that such a crime or treason has been perpetrated by the president. Last, two-thirds of the Duma and then two-thirds of the Federation Council within three months of each other must vote to impeach for the president to be removed. Moreover, with regards to legislature, the Duma and Federation Council can only override a presidential veto if two-thirds of both chambers approve (Staff of the Commission on Security and Cooperation in Europe 1994).

After almost two years of conflict, the distribution of power between the executive and legislative branches of government in Russia was resolved with the use of a referendum approving a new constitution. The constitution approved by the December 1993 referendum remains to date the Constitution of the Russian Federation. Russia, essentially now a presidential republic, has gone through two election cycles for president in 1996 and 2000 and for parliament in 1995 and 1999.

It is worth noting that Yeltsin's draft constitution was the last of a long sequence of alternative draft constitutions that had been fought over endlessly. In fairness, Yeltsin's referendum was also an attempt to end what otherwise would have been fruitless bargaining over a multitude of issues, for example the federal structure, the powers of the presidency versus the parliament, individual rights, and the role of the Communist Party.

The April 1993 referendums were, as with all the referendums discussed so far, initiated by the executive, but unlike any of the preceding cases, the legislature decided to fight back in earnest. Though the French Parliament attempted to resist de Gaulle, it was both too weak institutionally and too weak in public support to mount an effective resistance. In Russia, resistance by the Congress of People's Deputies before the 1993 votes took the form of refusing to have the referendums, limiting the extraordinary constitutional powers of the Russian president, and finally imposing its own wording in the questions. Resistance afterward took the form of refusing to allow new elections to be held for the Congress because of the supposed ambiguity of the results. In this case, the referendums made manifest, and may have exacerbated, a fundamental rift between Yeltsin and the Congress.

CHAPTER 5

Patterns in the Use of Referendums

Taken as a whole the referendums in France, Chile, the Soviet Union, and the Post-Soviet states provide insights that demonstrate not only continuities but emphasize unexpected results in the understanding of referendum politics. Trends established by cases often lead to conclusions about the effectiveness, and limits, of leadership, and why policy referendums, as opposed to the more numerous autonomy and constitutional votes, may become more important in the future. Toward this effort this chapter will explore the following arguments:

(1) Referendums are part of a bargaining process between elites who have their basis of power in different institutional settings.

(2) Referendums give political actors the political legitimacy to pursue change and potentially alter status quo institutions.

(3) Executives can better position themselves than legislatures along a policy spectrum to win when introducing referendums.

The third argument suggests several hypotheses that may be tested with the Large-N Data Set in this chapter.

(3.1) If executives can better position themselves along a policy spectrum, they should propose a greater number of referendums than legislatures.

(3.2) If executives can better position themselves along a policy spectrum, they should win a greater number of referendums than legislatures.

The evidence from the Large-N Data Set in support of the two hypotheses 3.1 and 3.2 suggests a marginally valid but broader story. Executives do use the referendum a considerable amount, but legislatures and other actors are capable of using this device as well when their positions better match the sentiment of the people or when taking on other intransigent institutions. Often lacking executives in 1991–1992, legislatures in the Soviet and Post-Soviet states used referendums to push for autonomy for their geographical units. Executives have proven to be more successful than others in using the referendum but legislatures have also had considerable success.

An analysis of referendum subjects over time reveals some interesting insights into transitions. Referendum subjects during transitions have been concerned more so with the distribution of power among state institutions and between the federal center and regions than with policy matters. There is a suggestion but no clear evidence that policy referendums will become more numerous than referendums dealing with autonomy and constitution once regimes begin to consolidate.

This analysis, however, will begin with a summary of evidence presented so far in the French, Chilean, Soviet, and Russian cases in chapters 2, 3, and 4 and a comparative look at their leadership. It will then turn to shorter case studies of how the referendum was used in the Ukraine, the Crimea, and Kyrgyzstan to show that the generalizations made from the French, Chilean, Soviet, and Russian cases do apply. This chapter will then present evidence from the Large-N Data Set for the two hypotheses concerning the executive use of the referendums in the Post-Soviet states and what referendum subjects reveal about transitions. It will then end with a brief discussion of referendum violence.

Summary of Referendum Cases to this Point: France, Chile, the Soviet Union, and Russia

Executives have been the chief initiators of the referendum device in the cases described so far. Opponents of these referendums have been legislatures, parties, the people, the military, and the republics. The military has often played an especially significant role. The military played an important role in the two Chilean referendums and also played a significant role in the 1993 Russian referendums. Moreover, the military as an actor was heavily involved in the issues if not the specific events of the French Algerian referendums. Although the military has been involved in many of these cases, the referendum device has resolved far more crises than it has exacerbated. Referendums have resolved issues in which the military was directly involved and situations in which the executive has miscalculated the political landscape and been forced to step aside (see table 5.1).

Table 5.1 Summary of referendum cases to this point: what have we learned?

Referendum (number of questions)	Actors (initiator underlined)	Perception of initiator	Elite opponent mobilized?	Crisis resolved?
France 1958 (1) Constitution	Executive, legislature	Correct	None	Yes
France 1961 (1) Alg. autonomy	Executive, legislature	Correct	None	Yes
France (1) 1962 Alg. agreement	Executive, legislature	Correct	None	Yes
France (1) 1962 Direct election of president	Executive, legislature	Correct	Legislature	Yes
France 1969 (1) Reduce power of Senate	Executive, legislature	Overoptimistic	Legislature	Yes
Chile 1973 (1) Econ. program	Executive, legislature, military	Correct*	Military	No
Chile 1988 (1) Extend Pinochet's term as president	Executive, military	Overoptimistic	People (Parties)	Yes
USSR 1991 (1) Approve union treaty	Executive, legislature, republic elite	Overoptimistic	Republic elite	No
Russia 1993 (4) Support for Yeltsin, econ. program, new elections for exec. and legislature	Executive, legislature	Correct	Legislature	No

* It is not completely clear what question Allende would have asked and, thus, not completely clear how well Allende perceived the situation in Chile.

In telling these stories, several themes have made themselves evident. First, executives use referendums to increase their power versus others. Second, executives seem to have an advantage with regard to using referendums because the people are often positioned closer to executives than to the groups with which executives are competing for power. Nevertheless, executives may misperceive their popularity and their ability to win and subsequently lose. Third, the subjects of these referendums are often constitutional—the distribution of power between institutions within a state—but may also deal with autonomy—the independence of geographic subunits from a federal state. Fourth, referendum opponents are usually legislatures but may also be the military, the people or political parties, and geographical subunits of states. Subregional concerns are often very different from the concerns of the federal center; moreover, autonomy referendums are often driven by ethnicity. For these reasons, autonomy referendums can be dangerous and devastating for executives. Fifth, if executives are opposed in a referendum campaign by an opponent with nearly equal power, referendums may reveal, or possibly exacerbate, conflict between executives and their opponents. Even if the referendum results are in an executive's favor, an executive may not have enough legitimacy and/or power to implement the results. Executives may ultimately need other support such as the military. Finally, *carryover* institutions, like the Russian Congress of People's Deputies, have their origins in pre-transition regimes and have views that are out of step with the transitioning polity and society. Though executives can outflank these institutions, *carryover* institutions can present a major obstacle for a reform effort.

Comparing Leaders in the Use of the Referendum Device

How do Gorbachev, Yeltsin, de Gaulle, and Pinochet compare and contrast with one another in the use of the referendum device? (See table 5.2.) Most used the referendum as a way to consolidate their power and win policy disputes by using the legitimacy of the people. Most also used the referendum device to get around their elite opposition, which

Table 5.2 Comparison of the use of the referendum device by Gorbachev, Yeltsin, de Gaulle, and Pinochet

Issue	Leader			
	Gorbachev	*Yeltsin*	*De Gaulle*	*Pinochet*
Goal of referendum	Reform/ increase power	Reform/ increase power	Reform/ increase power	Extend term in office/ legitimacy
Defeat elite?	Yes	Yes	Yes	No
Forced to call vote?	No	No	No	Yes
Leader good at strategy?	No	No	Yes	Yes
Leader good at tactics?	Yes	Yes	No	No
Leader's perception of referendum use?	Tool	Tool	Tool, connection to the people	Tool
Referendum subjects	1 autonomy 0 constitutional 0 policy	0 autonomy 6 constitutional 0 policy	2 autonomy 3 constitutional 0 policy	0 autonomy 2 constitutional 1 policy
Referendums won	1 out of 1; 100%	6 out of 6*; 100%	4 out of 5; 75%	2 out of 3; 67%
Loss ends regime?	—	—	Yes	Yes

* The Russian April 1993 referendum had four questions and is counted as four separate referendums.

was usually located in the legislature. Pinochet is the one exception to these two points primarily because his opposition came in the form of a mass movement. Pinochet also was the only one of these four leaders who was forced by the military to accept a negative referendum result he may have otherwise wanted to suspend. In the "mechanical" use of the referendum, Gorbachev and Yeltsin exhibited tactical strengths—political maneuvering that fulfills short-term goals sometimes at the expense of long-term objectives. De Gaulle and Pinochet were good at strategy—political maneuvering that leads to the fruition of long-term objectives. All four of these leaders, however, saw the referendum as a tool to be used to have their institutional power and policy issues decided. De Gaulle also seemed to be genuinely interested in connecting with the people through this device. Interestingly enough, it was also de Gaulle, along with Pinochet, who was forced to resign as a direct result of a negative referendum outcome. And maybe most telling of all, only two out of the twelve referendums that these men were responsible for actually dealt with purely policy issues and not the distribution of power between institutions or regions.

Mikhail Gorbachev, general secretary of the Communist Party of the Soviet Union from 1985 to 1991, made history when he called the first and only referendum in the Soviet Union's history. In fact, the referendum involved the most people ever in a democratic vote. Gorbachev called a vote on the approval of a new union treaty that would bind the Soviet republics together in a centralized union. From the perspective of many political reformers and the republics the measure did not go far enough in granting independence. Though Gorbachev won the vote, his action spawned many counter-referendums in the republics. Lithuania, Latvia, and Estonia held and won referendums on independence. Kirghizia, Uzbekistan, and Ukraine held referendums calling for status as "equal sovereign republics." Russia, on behalf of Yeltsin, held and passed the most influential referendum when it approved the office of president of Russia. Three months later the Russian people elected Yeltsin the first president of Russia. In negotiations with the republics later that summer, Gorbachev granted the Soviet republics greater autonomy from the center but not independence. From the perspective of conservatives within the Communist Party, however, these concessions were seen as a slippery slope that may have gone too far in granting autonomy for the republics.

With the March 1991 referendum on the union, Gorbachev was trying to regain control of a reform process that had spun out of his grasp. Though Gorbachev wanted reforms, he chiefly wanted them in order to increase the viability and vitality of the USSR economically, socially, and politically. In this context he proposed devolving some decision-making power back to the people primarily so that he could make more conservative members of the Party and bureaucracy heed his economic initiatives. He never wanted to see the Soviet state dissolve. Even though he wanted some degree of political liberty, he was never a pure Western democrat. He was a true democratic socialist in the tradition of a more liberally minded Lenin. Therefore, when some Soviet republics began demanding their independence on the grounds of self-determination—the principle he proclaimed as valid when he let the East European states exit the Communist bloc—he used the referendum device to show that the "people" of the USSR actually wanted to retain the union. Though he won the referendum, many republics either boycotted the vote, added their own question, changed his wording of the question, and/or called their own referendum; only four republics held the vote as he had asked.[1]

Boris Yeltsin, the first elected president of Russia, also used the referendum to defeat his political enemies. His education with the referendum device began in opposition to Gorbachev and the union treaty. Yeltsin sought greater Russian autonomy from the Soviet apparatus but could not mount a successful opposition to Gorbachev's March 1991 referendum. Instead, Yeltsin held a referendum on the same day within the Russian republic asking its citizens whether or not it desired a directly elected president. In doing so, Yeltsin orchestrated a political coup that culminated in him being elected the first democratic leader of Russia in its history. Yeltsin now enjoyed a very significant base of power with which to engage Gorbachev and the Soviet apparatus. His position as president of Russia gave him enough legitimacy to thwart the plotters of the Soviet August Coup attempt and demand from Gorbachev afterwards the essential dismantling of the Soviet state.

Yeltsin also used the referendum to further his goals and positions and defeat his political enemies within Russia after the fall of Communism. After several years, the opposition to Yeltsin's economic and social reforms became more powerful and aggressive within the legislature. When it reached the point where government business failed to get done, Yeltsin suggested the use of the referendum device to ask the people to adopt a new constitution that would dismantle the current legislature and create a presidential republic. Several months later, the legislature gave its final approval to a referendum but only after it had modified the questions with the goal of defeating Yeltsin. Nevertheless Yeltsin still won the votes. Four questions were called and all of them went his way.

The Russian people gave Yeltsin both a vote of confidence in him as their president and in his economic policies. A majority did not ask for early elections for Yeltsin, though it was close. Though a majority of those voting did approve early parliamentary elections, it was not a majority of the electorate.

Charles de Gaulle of France was the most skilled user of the referendum device in the latter half of the twentieth century and through its use may have strengthened the post–World War II French state. He used the referendum not only to defeat his political enemies and weaken the French legislature but also to receive the personal approval of the French people. After World War II, de Gaulle sought to remake the French state into a presidential republic in part because he blamed the ineffectiveness of the Fourth Republic upon parliamentary ineptitude. Thus he called one referendum on the direct election of the president in order to bypass Parliament. Another referendum was called on the devolution of power away from the Senate. De Gaulle in his remarks to the public always linked his personal legitimacy to that of the referendum and suggested—if he did not clearly say—that he would resign if the public did not vote for his position. In this way, de Gaulle turned every referendum vote into a referendum on himself. De Gaulle needed to connect with the French people and regularly confirm their confidence in him. In this way he lived and died by the referendum vote: he resigned after the vote to devolve power away from the Senate failed in April 1969.

Augusto Pinochet attempted to manipulate the referendum device three times before he also was forced to resign after unfavorable results. General Pinochet ruled Chile for over 15 years after a military junta he was part of overthrew its democratically elected government in 1973. Pinochet's regime held two referendums—in 1978 and 1980 respectively—both of which are considered by experts to have been conducted unfairly (Spooner 1994, 153–5; Oppenheim 1993). The referendum of 1988 would have allowed him to remain in office without being directly elected for another term. Pinochet had come to believe that a majority of the people supported his regime largely because of the relative success of the economy under his rule. The Chilean people however could not put aside the murders and human-rights violations that his regime had been responsible for since the coup. All observers in hindsight should have expected that Pinochet would attempt to remain in power by force irrespective of the referendum results. When the results did turn out against his continuation in power, Chile's military leaders refused to buttress his regime forcing Pinochet to step down.

Continuity in Post-Soviet Cases: Referendums in Kyrgyzstan, the Ukraine, and the Crimea

Further cases from the Post-Soviet states illustrate the same referendum politics observed in France, Chile, the Soviet Union, and Russia. Leaders from Kyrgyzstan, Ukraine, and the Crimea follow the same patterns as leaders in the earlier cases. In Kyrgyzstan and the Ukraine, leaders attempted to strengthen the executive at the expense of the legislature. Referendums proposed within the Ukraine's Crimean region asked for the same independence the Ukrainian Soviet Socialist Republic itself won from the Soviet Union.

If there is any difference it has been in the relative amount of success various countries and regions have had in their referendum efforts. Kyrgyz President Akayev was very successful in securing his goals but Ukrainian Presidents Kravchuk and Kuchma have faced stiffer competition from the legislature. The Crimea has not been successful in its bid to secede from the Ukraine; the Ukrainian SSR in 1991 faced a much weaker central foe in the delegitimized and collapsing Soviet Union.

Kyrgyzstan: President Akayev's Love Affair with the Referendum

One is immediately struck by the similarity between the series of referendums in Kyrgyzstan by Akayev and the Russian referendums in 1993 by Yeltsin. Akayev called a referendum to express a vote of confidence in himself and his economic reforms much like the ones held on Yeltsin in April 1993. After the Kyrgyz Parliament refused to participate in the work of the Supreme Council, Akayev called for new parliamentary elections and a referendum to reform the legislative branch of government as Yeltsin did in December 1993. Furthermore, Akayev, after winning reelection in December 1995, called for another referendum in early 1996 to consolidate even more executive power unto himself. The democrat who began reforms in Kyrgyzstan in 1992 seemed to have established at the very least rule by the executive by the beginning of 1996.

A referendum was held in Kyrgyzstan on Sunday, January 30, 1994 for a "vote of confidence"[2] in President Askar Akayev and his shock-therapy economic reforms. President Akayev is the only head of state of the five former communist central Asian republics who was never a communist leader and who enjoys a reputation as a good democrat.[3] By winning the "vote of confidence," Akayev could remain in office another two years up to 1996. The importance of the referendum vote was expressed well by Medetbay Sherimkulov, chairman of the Supreme Council:[4] "This is the first referendum since Kyrgyzstan became an independent state. It is important because if the nation expresses confidence in Askar Akayev his term of office will last until 1996. It is not only showing confidence in Akayev, but also giving the leadership an opportunity for another two years to continue to implement reform. If the reform is implemented, we can move forward. It means we will not reverse course or deviate from it . . . Frankly, we have many problems in the economy. We have to bring our laws in line with the process of reform."[5] President Akayev began the then current economic reforms in July of 1992. The reforms were begun in conjunction with the International Monetary Fund. He stated early his belief that the economy would stabilize by the end of 1992, but 1993 was a bad year for most Kyrgyz as inflation still ran at 1,600 percent while national income fell by 17 percent and unemployment surged. The average monthly salary at the time of the referendum vote was 135 soms, or about USD15, where 100 soms was considered subsistence level.[6]

Therefore, President Akayev was seen as taking a gamble by having the vote. Some accused the president of handing out political favors in order to win votes when he recently had stated his readiness to grant dual citizenship to Russians and Germans, one-quarter of the electorate.[7] He also seemed to be counting on Boris Yeltsin's support and a visit from the Russian president on the eve of the election.[8]

Results of the referendum vote contrast starkly with polling done beforehand. The Kyrgyz Central Electoral Commission stated that 2,176,000 or 95.9 percent of all eligible voters participated and 96.3 voted positively expressing confidence in Akayev.[9] Polling done by the "Sotsiomarket" Research Center around January 13 showed significant public opposition to Akayev: 46.4 percent did not approve of the referendum in principle, approximately 25 percent were prepared to vote against Akayev, 38.9 percent believed the republic is heading into a crisis while 29.3 responded that a crisis stage had already been reached.[10]

On Monday, January 31, 1994, the day after the vote, presidential press secretary, Imankadyr Rysaliyev, rejected accusations from the press that the results had been forged.[11] He noted that representatives from all the Kyrgyz political parties and movements, foreign diplomats, and journalists monitored the vote. Rysaliyev stressed, "Not a single representative said anything about some pressure or violations of generally recognized rules of referendum ... The turnout at the referendum and Akayev's success showed that the Kyrgyz people have rallied behind the acknowledged leader—Askar Akayev."[12] I have found no conclusive evidence of the results of this referendum being forged beyond the circumstantial evidence provided by the ultra-high percent turnout and "yes" vote.

Forged referendum results provide a problem for analysis. Should forged vote results be handled differently? On one hand these votes do not differ significantly from votes that have been highly manipulated by other means and simply may differ as a matter or degree. Manipulated votes suffer the most with respect to their legitimacy from the perspective of the people and the referendum opponents; forged vote results have a similar but much more intense legitimacy problem. Any regime capable and willing to forge the results of a referendum vote are likely to already have a monopoly on the use of force whether or not force is actually used, for example Chile under Pinochet during the 1988 referendum. Therefore it is unlikely if forged results as the sole factor will lead to greater instability even though the referendum opponents have even greater justification to participate in civil disobedience.

President Akayev seemed determined to reap the benefits of winning the referendum. Press Secretary Rysaliyev also stated on the day after the vote that "The success at the referendum necessitates sharp radicalization of reforms, and they will follow."[13] A week later, Akayev mentioned that the referendum results confirmed his policy of interethnic accord, and that he would use the referendum results to "strengthen all branches of power and to coordinate their activities to work efficiently for solving the most important problems of the society."[14] To that end the same day he signed two decrees entitled "On Urgent Measures on Strengthening State and Financial Discipline" and "On Urgent Measures on Strengthening Law and Order and Reinforcing the Fight Against Infringers of the Law."[15]

The October 1994 referendum on amendments to the Kyrgyz Constitution resulted from a dramatic parliamentary crisis. One hundred and forty-three out of the 323 members of the Kyrgyz Parliament refused to attend its last session because they stated, "the parliament had become a stage for political struggle and intrigues and [had] lost credibility with the people"[16] and had become "a scene of political haggling and unproductive discussions."[17] Many members gave speeches on how they believed democracy was threatened if not dead in their country.[18] President Akayev then convinced the government,[19] or cabinet, to resign citing the Constitution on how the government could not outlast the Parliament.[20] Akayev then issued an edict in which he not only called for new parliamentary elections in 1994 but also a referendum on amending the Constitution. Following is the wording of the referendum and the amendments he sought to adopt:

> Do you agree that the following clauses should be incorporated into Sections 1 and 2 of Chapter 1 of the Constitution of the Kyrgyz Republic:
> i. Amendments and addenda to the Constitution of the Kyrgyz Republic and to laws of the Kyrgyz Republic, as well as other important problems of state life, may be put to a referendum? (Yes/No)
> ii. Legislative authority in the Kyrgyz Republic is carried out by the Zhogorku Kenesh [Supreme Council] consisting of two chambers—the Legislative Assembly [zakonodatelnoye sobraniye] with 35 deputies, a standing body elected to represent the interests of the republic's entire population; and the Assembly of People's Representatives [sobraniye narodnykh predstavitely] with 70 deputies, which works in session and is elected to represent territorial interests. (Yes/No)[21]

In this way, President Akayev meant to divide and weaken Parliament much as Yeltsin did with the December 1993 *constitutional* referendum in Russia. Akayev argued, as Yeltsin and de Gaulle did before him, that a strong state requires a strong executive and weakened legislature. By reinforcing the power of the referendum device and reforming Parliament into a bicameral legislature, President Akayev meant to change the distribution of power between institutions to favor the executive and diminish the legislature.

President Akayev has clearly stated his fondness for the referendum device and its central place in Kyrgyz politics. In a nationwide address, he stated, "the referendum in Kyrgyzstan is objectively becoming one of the most real and effective forms of democracy."[22] Moreover, he believes that the use of the referendum device is consistent with "the mentality of our people and certain psychological traits of the national character."[23] He claims to believe that the "people" have a central, guiding role in a democracy and that free elections and referendums are "the supreme direct expressions of people's power."[24]

In fact, he puts the "power of the people" above that of the legislature. He justifies this position by claiming that key clauses were omitted from the Kyrgyz Constitution adopted by the Supreme Council because the Parliament had been looking out for its own interests.[25] Instead, he argues that the Constitution should have been approved by a Constitutional Assembly and put to a referendum vote much like it was done in Estonia, Lithuania, Latvia, and Russia. He gives the following explanation: "It is clear that none of these constitutions gives the people a back-seat role or replaces them with the parliament. I have no wish to overdramatize the situation that has arisen here, but judge for yourselves: By the will of our parliamentarians the people have been excluded from being a subject of the constitutional process, to put it in legal language. A national referendum was not named as one of the ways of changing the Constitution. The parliamentarians think that only they are worthy of this great mission."[26]

President Akayev in another speech addressed not only the national Kyrgyz audience but also a Western and international one as well in defense of his recent statements on the press and the suspension of Parliament. He claimed to want to hold the "opposition," or Parliament, to the same requirements that government is subject to, which in this instance he describes as the "requirements of the law, the requirements of justice and the requirements of morality."[27] Similarly he talks about "elementary loyalty to the legitimate opposition" or as he also puts it the "Western concept of a loyal opposition."[28] By this he means, somewhat understandably, that members of the opposition were brought up in the Communist system where they did not learn how to properly tolerate political rivals. He describes the parliamentary opposition as being unable to acknowledge the role that a government and its opposition play in democracy and the "fundamental values" they all should share.[29] Akayev's stated hope was to fix this situation by using the referendum to pass the above constitutional amendments concerning Parliament and the general use of the referendum.

Akayev's words must have proven convincing for the people of the Kyrgyz Republic. For the first clause 84.9 percent voted positively allowing future constitutional amendments and changes to Kyrgyz laws to be made by referendum. For a bicameral legislature 84 percent voted positively with a permanent sitting upper house and lower working body that meets in sessions. In the referendum on October 22, 1994 86.4 percent of all eligible voters participated.[30] It is also worth noting that the referendum vote was combined with elections to local councils. This was done, says Akayev, to cut down on costs but it also probably contributed to the high voter turnout.

Once again some observers challenged the validity of the referendum vote. In an open letter to the Kyrgyz Supreme Court, the presidium of the Political Council and the Council of the Bishkek city organization of the Democratic Party of Free Kyrgyzstan stated that there were three kinds of violations: "(1) A large number of voters received ballot papers without producing their passports and, as a result, the same people voted several times; (2) Many people voted in behalf of their relatives and this was allowed openly by the heads of the polling station commissions despite protests from observers and agents; (3) A great number of ballot papers were placed in ballot boxes on the pretext they contained proxy votes."[31] Nevertheless the validity of the vote was upheld by the Kyrgyz Central Electoral Committee.[32]

The next referendum, proposed by 50 members of the new Kyrgyz Parliament on April 3, 1995, would extend the term of office of President Akayev until the year 2001 and thus bypass presidential elections set for the fall of 1996. It is likely that Akayev orchestrated this referendum; if he did, he also put on a very good show denying any interest in the vote. Presidential Press Secretary Kamil Bayalinov quoted Akayev saying that such a referendum could not be held without the proper legislative basis. Another member of the president's staff was quoted as saying that Akayev under no circumstances would accept a referendum extending his term.[33] In response to the signature collection, the upper house of Parliament proposed on August 21 an amendment to the law on referendums disallowing the extension of terms of office for presidents and parliamentary deputies. By September 11, over a million signatures, about half of the electorate, had been collected. Nevertheless, the Legislative Assembly voted on September 20 not to hold the referendum by a margin of 30 to 3.[34] This came in the wake of a group of four political parties and seven NGOs beginning a hunger strike on September 18 in protest of the proposed referendum. But the election for president did happen on December 24, 1995 and not the next fall as had been expected.

President Akayev suggested several more referendums whose purpose seemed to be to manipulate the political and electoral process further. Along with this early presidential election, Akayev also suggested that a referendum be held on whether Russian should have the same status as the Kyrgyz language. Such a suggestion seems to have been an obvious attempt to appeal to the Russian-as-first-language population for their vote in the presidential election. After reelection, Akayev on January 3, 1996 went on to propose a referendum that would remedy as he saw it a "vacuum of power and responsibility" by establishing a constitutional basis for the separation of powers.[35]

In conclusion, President Akayev adeptly used the referendum device to develop a presidential, as opposed to parliamentary, republic as de Gaulle and Yeltsin did before him. Like de Gaulle before him, President Akayev talked of the need to bring the "people" more directly into the political process into a position superior to that of the legislature. In many ways, President Akayev may have had even more success than both de Gaulle and Yeltsin when one considers that his hold on power has been solidified electorally and stood stronger than Yeltsin's last years of office in Russia.

Ukraine: Kravchuk and Kuchma Attempt to Strengthen the Executive by Referendum

The Ukraine presents referendum cases that clearly show the bargaining and conflict among political elites in executive and legislative institutions. *Constitutional* referendums that strengthen the executive at the expense of the legislature have been proposed in the Ukraine, France, Russia, Kyrgyzstan, and throughout the Post-Soviet area. The Ukrainian cases are somewhat different compared with France and Kyrgyzstan and more like Russia in 1993 because the Ukrainian legislature and executive had relatively equal power and legitimacy. The Ukrainian presidents have had less success against parliament than the French, Kyrgyz, and even Russian counterparts making for an interesting case study.

Like Russian President Yeltsin and Kyrgyz President Akayev, Ukrainian Presidents Kravchuk and Kuchma attempted to strengthen the executive vis-à-vis the legislature by proposing referendums. In their view, the task of reforming their countries required a strong executive: divided government and significant compromise on legislation did not lend itself to bold, decisive reforms. Moreover, public confidence in reform leaders usually eroded over time as marketeering measures decreased the standard of living. Historically, few leaders who usher in significant change ever survive politically, even literally, as it is usual for a backlash against them to occur unless they control significant, almost dictatorial power—that is, Attaturk in Turkey. The attempt to centralize power in the presidency was perceived by legislative leaders in most Post-Soviet states, however, as an executive power grab and a threat to democracy. What is clear is that after the Russian referendums of 1993 and Yeltsin's stated success in them, the chief executives of other Post-Soviet states had a historical precedent to follow. They had reason to believe that the referendum process would work out in their favor because rarely had an executive "lost" a referendum vote.

So it should have come as no surprise that President Kravchuk in his 1994 New Year's address to Ukrainians proposed the idea of holding a referendum on the "Law on Authority." Unlike in Russia, a new constitution could not be submitted for approval to the people through a referendum. Nevertheless, the vote on a law on authority would serve the same end: a positive vote would act as a vote of confidence in Kravchuk and make discussion of early presidential elections moot. More similarly, Ivan Stepanovich, the chairman of the Ukrainian Parliament—the Supreme Council—was opposed to holding a referendum because either he feared a referendum vote would decrease the power of the legislature and/or he himself had aspirations for the presidency and wanted early elections to the office to permit himself to run.[36] According to the current law, only Parliament was authorized to adopt a new constitution. The extended Supreme Council debate on new constitutional provisions and a referendum to decide a new "law on authority" never materialized into a vote.

What did materialize was legislation passed by the Supreme Council in March 1994 giving local councils all executive authority and eliminating regional presidential envoys. New elections to local councils were scheduled for June 26 and afterwards the new law was designed to go into effect. Such an obvious usurpation of the president's power led Kravchuk to state, "the president would then effectively cease to be head of the Executive Branch."[37] In light of the indeterminate nature of presidential powers at that moment, Kravchuk said he would not seek another term in office by contesting the presidential election on June 26.[38]

This executive–legislative standoff over political reforms continued into President Kuchma's term of office. Kuchma feared that parliamentary intransigence was harming his ability to implement economic reforms. In April 1995, the Ukrainian Parliament had given his government, or cabinet, a vote of no confidence. Before Kuchma would attempt to nominate a new cabinet, he wanted a draft constitutional bill on the separation of powers between the executive and legislature to be passed that would allow him to implement economic reforms more easily. On May 13, 1995, President Kuchma threatened to hold a nonbinding referendum on the separation of powers if Parliament failed to pass his bill.[39] Kuchma prevailed—the Ukrainian Parliament voted to accept a compromise bill on the separation of power on May 18 that included the following: the president would have sole authority to form a government, or cabinet, without parliament's approval of key ministers; however, the president's ability to call a referendum was now limited to "issues related to the adoption of a new post-Soviet constitution."[40]

Executive–legislative conflict continued in the Ukraine, however. On May 31, 1995, Parliament vetoed President Kuchma's decree on holding a nonbinding referendum on confidence in him and Parliament. This prompted Kuchma to reissue on June 5 the decree on holding the referendum on June 28.[41] On November 12, 1995, Kuchma threatened to call a referendum himself on his draft constitution if Parliament did not agree to hold the vote. His version of the constitution, of course, instituted a strong executive. Kuchma called the left-wing attempt to abolish the presidency and make Ukraine a parliamentary republic a "disaster."[42]

In conclusion, even though Kravchuk and Kuchma had less success than Akayev, their goals were the same. Kravchuk and Kuchma wanted to strengthen the executive at the expense of the legislature, but in the case of the Ukraine, the Parliament was much stronger than the one in Kyrgyzstan and even Russia. Nevertheless, the executive did use the referendum with some success. Moreover the Ukraine had other issues with which to deal—most importantly, the autonomy movement in the Crimea.

Crimean Autonomy *Referendums*

The most complicated and long-lasting independence movement in the Post-Soviet states has been that of the Crimea in the Ukraine. Leaders of the Crimea have proposed a variety of referendums aimed at greater independence and a few have taken place. The politics of independence in the Crimea makes it an excellent case to illustrate *autonomy* referendums in the Post-Soviet states.

The complex history of the Crimea and Ukraine has not helped the actors involved resolve the issue of Crimean independence. The Ukraine had been faced with the issue of Crimean independence before the dissolution of the Soviet Union. The Crimea only became part of the Ukraine, then the Ukrainian SSR, in 1954; beforehand it had been an integral part of Russia. It is home to a Russian majority that historically has had close ties to Moscow. The Crimea is also home to ethnic Ukrainians and Tartars. Since 1992, the Russian majority, represented by the Crimean government, has advocated Crimean independence from Ukraine and integration into Russia; the Crimean Ukrainians and Tartars have resisted the secession move. The Ukrainian government has been indignant toward the Crimean government's secessionist movement and has deemed their actions as unconstitutional.

The Russian nationalist majority in the Crimea is a good example of how majority groups in subareas try to use referendums to increase their power. The cohesiveness of these majority groups is usually based upon ethnicity of which language and religion can be important components. A common pattern often repeated is not only of majority groups in subareas of a country trying to increase their power but also that these groups may share an ethnic bond with the people of a neighboring country that they do not share with the people within their own countries. In the latter case, both ethnic majorities and minorities can have cross-border or transnational connections that complicate the domestic politics of the countries involved.

On January 20, 1991, in the last year of the Soviet Union, a referendum proposed by the Russian-speaking majority was held to decide whether Crimea would become an autonomous republic within the Ukraine. It was boycotted *en masse* by the Tartars of the region. Some have argued that the Crimean authorities went to some length to prevent the Tartars from expressing their overwhelming negative vote. The Tartar-language newspaper *Dostluk* was not distributed on the Saturday before the vote and did not reappear until Tuesday.[43] Nevertheless, it was reported that the "Crimean ASSR" had been restored by an overwhelming vote. Ukrainian President Kravchuk even pronounced the results as "just."[44] After the demise of the USSR, however, the Crimea lost its semiautonomous status and reverted back to Ukraine proper.

The Republican Movement of Crimea (RDK), which favored the peninsula's return to Russia, made two serious referendum proposals for Crimea's secession from Ukraine. The first attempt in November 1991 was ruled illegal because there was no law on referendums on the books at the time.[45] The second attempt by the RDK successfully gathered by April 1, 1992, the 180,000 signatures needed to hold the vote; in fact, 250,000 signatures were collected.[46] Ukrainian President Kravchuk warned the Crimean lawmakers and people against supporting the referendum, saying the vote was being promoted by those attempting to set "Russia against Ukraine by playing the Crimean card."[47] Kravchuk stated that the Crimea would retain much of its autonomy and promised that there would be no forced Ukrainization, but that the rights of the Crimea's Ukrainian and Tartar minorities needed to be respected. This statement highlighted one of the wrinkles in Crimean politics and one of the questionable parts of the Soviet Union's history: Stalin, in 1944, deported most of the Crimean Tartars to Central Asia for allegedly collaborating with the Nazis (Commission on Security and Cooperation in Europe 1994). Kravchuk stated his continued support for the policy that was returning the Crimean Tartars to their homeland.[48] On May 5, the Crimean Parliament, based on a proposal from the RDK, passed a partial independence resolution that did not sever all ties with Ukraine. On May 6, the Parliament passed an amendment to the Constitution stating that though the Crimea is a part of the Ukraine, it would determine its "relations with Ukraine on the basis of treaties and agreements."[49] The independence vote was set for August 2.

The impending vote for independence began to raise tensions and the ire of Kiev. Besides the expected referendum question on the approval of the Crimean independence resolution passed by Parliament on May 5, a second referendum question, suggested by the RDK, asked whether voters supported a fully independent Crimea "in union with other states," meaning of course Crimea's return to Russia.[50] On May 13, the Ukrainian Parliament, clearly enraged, passed a resolution canceling Crimea's independence resolution, declared the August 2 referendum unconstitutional, and gave the Crimean Parliament one week to rescind its decision. Ukrainian parliamentary deputies demanded that the Crimean Parliament be dissolved, direct presidential rule be introduced, and that Nikolai Bagrov, chairman of the Crimean Parliament, "be held criminally responsible."[51] In response, the Crimean Parliament backed down; on May 21 it voted to rescind its independence resolution. On July 9 it voted to postpone indefinitely the August 2 referendum on independence citing the reason that it did not want the vote to interfere with its negotiations with the Ukrainian national government.[52] Because Moscow leaning Russian-speakers outnumber the Ukrainians and Tartars in the Crimea, the independence referendum, if held, would probably pass.

The suspended independence referendum did not deter the Crimean Russian nationalists for long, however. While pro-Ukrainian groups proposed a referendum dissolving the Parliament, pro-Moscow forces turned their energy toward instituting the position of president in the government of the Crimea. The pro-Ukrainian forces failed to have their referendum held while the pro-Moscow forces succeeded in influencing the Parliament to create the post of president and scheduling the first candidate election for January 16, 1994. The pro-Moscow, ethnic Russian candidate Yuri Meshkov won. He became the Crimea's first elected president and within months he proposed a new referendum to be held simultaneously with parliamentary elections on March 27, 1994. The referendum included three questions designed to give the Crimea *de facto* autonomy:

1. Are you for the restoration of the provision of the Constitution of the Republic of Crimea of 6 May 1992 which determines the regulation of mutual relations between the Republic of Crimea and Ukraine on the basis of a TREATY and AGREEMENTS? (Yes/No)
2. Are you for the restoration of the provision of the Constitution of the Republic of Crimea of 6 May 1992 that proclaimed the RIGHT OF CITIZENS OF THE REPUBLIC OF CRIMEA TO DUAL CITIZENSHIP? (Yes/No)
3. Are you for conceding the FORCE OF LAWS to the edicts of the president of the Republic of Crimea on questions that are temporarily not regulated by legislation of the Republic of Crimea? (Yes/No)[53]

However, pressure from Kiev forced Meshkov to downgrade the referendum to a nonbinding vote. Though Ukrainian President Kravchuk banned this consultative vote, it was held anyway. The results for the forementioned three questions were respectively: 1. 78.4 percent yes; 2. 82.8 percent yes; 3. 80 percent yes.[54]

Though the Crimean Parliament and various factions threatened to use the referendum device at least three more times, no further referendums have been held. In June 1994, the Crimean Parliament threatened to lift its ban on independence referendums if Kiev did not halt its interference with the Crimean militia. The Communist Party of Crimea announced in October 1994 a signature collecting campaign to hold a referendum on the dissolution of the Parliament; the Parliament had not been able to bring the Crimean Constitution in line with the Ukraine's and, on at least one occasion, had not been able to reach a quorum for business; the pro-Moscow faction that controlled Parliament had little desire to give in to Kiev. This conflict over the Constitution reached a head in the spring and summer of 1995. The last straw for Kiev came when several Crimean deputies threatened to hold a referendum on reunification with Russia. In response, the Ukrainian parliament annulled the Crimea's Constitution, abolished its presidency, decided to begin criminal proceedings against Meshkov, and moved to disarm his presidential guard.[55] Moreover, President Kuchma took temporary control of the local government. In an attempt to de-escalate, the Crimean Parliament decided not to hold a vote on the Crimea's independence if the Ukrainian Parliament reinstated the Crimean Constitution without the articles that conflicted with Ukraine's and reestablished the presidency. Final ratification of the Crimean Constitution by the Crimean and Ukrainian Parliaments, and more threats from both, dragged on well into 1996.

Evidence from the Large-N Data Set of the Soviet and Post-Soviet States

Although the cases presented so far have provided detailed and compelling evidence of how referendums have been used and their effects in specific instances, the Large-N Data Set of all referendums in the Soviet and Post-Soviet states allows us to answer different but no less important questions. The Soviet and Post-Soviet states are unique in that each former republic of the Soviet Union, though not entirely similar, have a shared history and set of legacies from the past—nearly identical political, economic, social, and cultural norms and institutions imposed by the Communist Party from Moscow. As a social scientific laboratory, the Large-N Data Set provides a solid foundation from which to provide even more evidence for some of the arguments put forward in this text. The value of the Large-N Data Set derives from the fact that it is comprehensive of all referendums in the Soviet and Post-Soviet states from 1990 to 1997 and referendum cases have a shared starting point in the Soviet Union. This data set included the entire set of 152 proposed and/or held referendums on the national, regional, and city levels in the Soviet and Post-Soviet states from 1990 to 1997.[56] This Large-N Data Set was created from an extensive, long-running research effort in which facts were collected and then rechecked against all available source material.[57]

Is There an Executive Advantage in Using the Referendum?

One of the arguments made throughout this work is that (3) executives can better position themselves than a legislature along a policy spectrum with respect to an issue in order to call and win a referendum more effectively. Most often this argument has been expressed in the case studies with spatial models that were based upon my own critical assessment of the political situation based sometimes on polls but mostly on the strategic maneuverings I have detailed. This work detailed two hypotheses to be tested in light of the above argument: (3.1) If executives can better position themselves along a policy spectrum, they should propose a greater number of referendums than legislatures; (3.2) If executives can better position themselves along a policy spectrum, they should win a greater number of referendums than legislatures. Let us now turn to the Large-N Data Set to see how this argument concerning the executive use of the referendum holds up against the aggregate evidence.

Out of 152 referendums, executives have proposed 53 but the legislature has proposed 58, political parties without majorities in Parliament have proposed 13, public initiative groups have proposed 10, while 18 referendums could not be reliably be coded by a specific initiator (see table 5.3). Out of these proposed referendums, executives actually held 33 out of 53 votes while the legislatures held 45 out of 58 votes. However, out of the referendums held, executives won 32 out of 33 votes while the legislatures only won 37 out of 45 votes. If we break the votes down by subject we find that in the category of autonomy votes, executives proposed 14, held 8, and won 8; legislatures proposed 32, held 27, and won 23. Of those 23 autonomy votes proposed and won by legislatures, it is important to note that 14 were held before most government bodies had executives in 1991 while only 9 have been held

Table 5.3 Crosstabulation of proposed referendums by subject with their specific initiators in the Post-Soviet states 1990–1997

Referendum subject	Specific initiator					
	?	Executive	Legislature	Political party (without parliamentary majority)	Public	Grand total
Autonomy	5	14	32	3	2	56
Constitutional	8	29	16	6	5	64
Policy	5	10	10	4	3	32
Grand total	18	53	58	13	10	152

since 1991. Among constitutional referendums, executives proposed 29, held 18, and won all 18; legislatures proposed 16, held 10, and won 9.[58] Among policy referendums, executives proposed 10, held 7, and won 6 while legislatures also proposed 10, held 8, and won 5.

The evidence is not immediately clear on whether or not executives are better than legislatures at positioning with respect to the people along a policy spectrum. Legislatures seem as eager as executives to call referendums; they called five more referendums than executives. However, these results are tempered by the fact that most government bodies in the Post-Soviet states did not have executives in 1991; they were mostly made up of soviets, or councils, on the republic, regional, and local levels. Nevertheless this data seems to show that legislatures at the very least did not feel uncomfortable with the referendum device. In the category of constitutional referendums, where executives and legislatures are likely to go head to head against one another, executives on the other hand did propose 29 votes while legislatures only proposed 16. This seems to say that executives felt more comfortable with their policy positions with respect to the people than the legislatures. Gross numbers do not support hypothesis 3.1, but a closer look at constitutional referendums reveal support for an executive advantage.

There is more evidence to support hypothesis 3.2, which argues that executives will win more referendums than legislatures because they can better position themselves along a policy spectrum. Executives won 32 out of 33, or 97 percent, of the referendums they proposed and held while legislatures won 37 out of 45, or 82 percent, of the votes they proposed and held. Executives won the entire set of constitutional and autonomy referendums they proposed and held; however, legislatures won nine out of ten of the constitutional referendums it proposed and held. The reasons for this statistic have been discussed already at length: the argument that the people are often closer to an executive than a legislature on any given issue because of the *carryover* nature of some legislative institutions in transitions that puts them out of step with the public; but also because of the ability of an executive to attract public sentiment and use the bully pulpit of their office in support of their cause; and the ability of the executive to choose the subject, wording, and timing of a referendum and interpret its results (see chapter 6).

The most numerous referendum subjects of leaders in the Post-Soviet states were *constitutional*: they made up 64 out of a total of 152, or 42 percent. Nearly every one of these referendums dealt with a change in the distribution of power between executive and legislative institutions. Strategically, the "people" seemed to side with the executives with respect to strengthening the executives and weakening the legislatures. Therefore executives have proposed referendums to take advantage of this sentiment by putting forth topics like a "vote of confidence," reforming parliament into a bicameral legislature, and granting additional powers to the executive. Referendum subjects, particularly constitutional and autonomy votes, have demonstrated a great deal of analytical purchase. There is a real distinction between different kinds of votes and it may be that we can learn something more about transitions if we take a closer look.

Autonomy and Constitutional Referendums

What kind of referendums would one expect from a country in a transition period? It seems reasonable that the issues at the heart of autonomy and constitutional referendums need to be resolved before policy questions can be meaningfully addressed. One might expect that leaders and elites vying for power in a transition would initiate referendums in order to secure their own legitimacy and the power of their respective institutions. Similarly, states and/or their geographical subunits would most likely concern themselves with their sovereign status sooner rather than later. Often, constitutional and autonomy issues surface before the formal beginning of a transition and likely serve as impetus for change to occur. The empirical evidence in the Large-N Data Set strongly supports this argument: there have been 56 autonomy referendums and 64 constitutional referendum for a grand total of 120 referendums out of 152 coded by subject to be constitutional and autonomy referendums in the Soviet and Post-Soviet transition.[59]

As countries begin to consolidate their regimes, the numbers of constitutional and autonomy referendums should therefore decrease. Most autonomy issues are resolved over time. As the power struggle within a country is resolved, actors may need to call fewer referendums with subjects—like strengthening executive power—that primarily affect their interests. Moreover, as civil society begins to flourish in a democratic polity, the general public may begin to become more active initiating their own referendums with subjects closer to their everyday interests like the economy without unleashing a struggle of power between domestic institutions.

The Large-N Data Set shows some evidence of autonomy referendums decreasing, but constitutional votes remain high and policy votes have barely increased over time (see figure 5.1). The absolute number of autonomy referendums has decreased from 20 per year in 1991 to 2 in 1996. Though constitutional referendums did begin to decrease in 1996, there is no conclusive evidence of a trend downwards as of spring of 1997. Though this study would argue that the number of constitutional referendums should begin to decrease over the years, they actually increased during four of the six years in this study. The relatively large number of constitutional referendums in 1996—ten—is more than the six policy referendums and two autonomy referendums. The evidence is inconclusive about the future number of policy referendums.

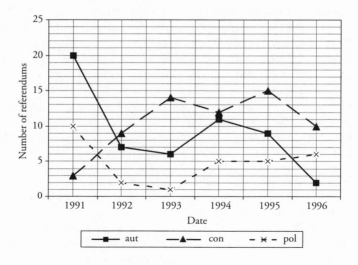

Figure 5.1 Number of referendums by subject in the Post-Soviet states 1991–1996

Policy referendums increased in numbers from 1993 through 1996 but only from one to six per year for the entire Post-Soviet region. What this data suggests is that basic issues about the structure of the state and the distribution of power between institutions were still very much undecided in the mid- to late 1990s.

A Closer Look at Autonomy Referendums

Though autonomy referendums make up 56 votes, eight less than constitutional referendums, it would be unwise to argue that they have been any less important. These referendums, as stated earlier, have justified the independence movements of many states. Gorbachev attempted to nullify the separatist desires of several states, especially the Baltics, by relegitimizing the Soviet empire with a referendum on a new union treaty. This referendum introduced the current usage of the referendum device into the Soviet and Post-Soviet states, and served as the initial impetus for the first independence votes of Soviet republics in January and February of 1991. It was also the impetus for the Russian referendum on establishing a presidency that spring, which allowed the new Russian president, Boris Yeltsin, to challenge Gorbachev for the leadership of the Russian people.

Most autonomy referendums have been proposed by republic legislatures with ethnicity sometimes playing a role. A significant portion of this legislative involvement can be traced back to the fact that most republics lacked executives outside of their Soviet, legislative structures during their original push for autonomy in 1991. In the Large-N Data Set, legislatures have proposed 32 out of 56 autonomy referendums. Executives have proposed 14, political parties without majority control in a legislature have proposed 3, and the public has proposed 2. Ethnicity played a role in every Soviet republic's autonomy or independence-related referendum in 1991; Slavic and non-Slavic republics alike attempted to distinguish themselves from Moscow. The only non-Slavic republic that failed to propose to use the referendum device in 1991 as a means to garner legitimacy at the expense of Moscow was Tajikistan. These ethnically inspired or justified independence movements gave rise to the expanded study of "nationalities" in Soviet and Post-Soviet area studies in the early 1990s. Of the former Soviet republics, only Russia, Belarus, and the Ukraine had majority-Slavic populations. Even so, the Ukraine held a counter-referendum in March 1991 on its autonomy and Russia held a referendum on instituting the presidency as a way to strengthen its position regarding the Soviet Union.

Autonomy referendums deal with a state's independence from or integration into a larger governmental body. A good example of a state's integration into a larger state or governing body would be Lukashenka's desire to see Belarus as a part of a greater Russian state. Autonomy referendums may also illustrate the process of *fission*—entities breaking up into smaller and smaller parts—that has been taking place in the Soviet and Post-Soviet region since the fall of Communism. Seventy percent, or 39 out of 56, of autonomy referendums have dealt with smaller entities seeking independence from larger ones that included them. When graphed by year from 1991 to 1995, the percentage of autonomy referendums involving fission decreases steadily. In 1996, though the two autonomy referendums both illustrated fission, this number of total referendums is very small and may not represent a legitimate challenge to the downward trend (see figure 5.2).

Referendums and Conflict

Though the Russian April 1993 referendums illustrate well how conflict can result from the strategic dynamic of referendum elite bargaining, very few referendums in this Large-N Data Set have ended in conflict.[60]

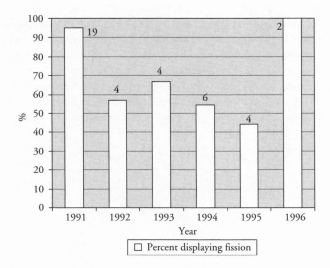

Figure 5.2 Percentage of autonomy referendums displaying fission by year with count displaying fission at top

Many more referendums, however, have been associated by subject matter with conflict or called to resolve a potential crisis. Autonomy referendums are rarely meek affairs, and most have had an implicit undercurrent of violence and institutional conflict. The Baltic independence movements from the USSR, and specifically the Lithuanian movement, existed in an atmosphere of violence and its threat from the Soviet central authorities until the USSR finally collapsed in the fall of 1991. Since 1991, the breakaway regions within Russia and Ukraine, and the referendums they have proposed, have been met stiffly by an implicit threat of violence if not its explicit use.

Outside of Russia in 1993, most Post-Soviet executives have been able to dominate opposition parliaments in various constitutional referendums and thus make the likelihood of violent conflict remote. President Askar Akayev of Kyrgyzstan, President Nursultan Nazarbaev of Kazakhstan, and Belorussian President Alyaksandr Lukashenka may be the best examples of executives dominating their political realm. This nonviolent record may be in danger if these leaders begin to lose referendums; however, the experiences of de Gaulle and Pinochet cast doubt on violence being the result of an executive losing a vote.

Policy referendums rarely affect the distribution of power between institutions, unlike autonomy and constitutional votes, so the likelihood of passions being inflamed enough for violence to occur seems minimal. The stakes simply are not high enough for actors in policy referendums for crises, much less violence, to occur. Policy referendums that touch upon highly controversial issues—like language laws or citizenry requirements—can bring in a factor, like ethnicity, that can result in the stakes being raised. These kinds of policy votes can even introduce another state actor—like Russia regarding the treatment of ethnic Russians in the Baltics—that could possibly introduce a threat of violence. Nevertheless, the likelihood of violence stemming from policy votes is very low.

CHAPTER 6

Pros and Cons of Referendums and Democratic Theory

By what method should the country express its decision? I reply: by the most democratic way, the referendum. It is also the most justified way, for national sovereignty belongs to the people and it belongs to it obviously, in the first instance, in the constitutional domain.

Charles de Gaulle, quoted in a televised speech on
September 20, 1962 in defense of his referendum proposal to elect the
French president directly by the people.

(Lacouture 1991, 490)

Why Referendums are So Attractive

The popularity of the referendum device never completely fades and periodically captures the political fortunes of a state. It has been used by both reforming and conservative forces as well as leaders who wished to direct a political outcome in the guise of democracy. The referendum device is one of the institutions of direct democracy that claim to measure and express the will of the people better than the institutions of representative democracy. Executives and legislatures, in their bid to out do the other, have utilized the referendum to secure their political goals. Moreover in most of these cases it has been at the impetus of an elite or elites that referendums have been called. And most often, executives—presidents, prime ministers, and dictators of various names—have suggested and called these votes. They have been particularly popular among authoritarian or authoritarian-minded leaders because of their susceptibility to abuse. Leaders can manipulate a referendum if they have the opportunity to decide whether or not the vote is called, its subject, its wording, the timing of the vote, and the chance to interpret the results. Thus the ultimate *vox populi* becomes the *vox caesaris*.

And not unlike the actual Caesar's controversial proclamations, speeches, and polls before the Roman polity, referendums have been controversial in how, when, why, and by whom they have been used. This device has been used to circumvent unresponsive legislatures and intransigent executives. It has been used in times of stability and transition, and has preceded, and followed, revolutions. The referendum device has been used to push through democratic reforms and to justify illiberal, antidemocratic regimes. It has also been used by individuals seeking power and by citizen groups seeking redress. Thus it is very hard to assign normative value to this device in general. Maybe the most that can be said about whether it is a "good" or "bad" institution is that it is neither; only the referendum sponsors themselves can be held to task for their intent.

Referendums have attracted the attention of politicians, citizens, and scholars alike because of their claim to express the people's will. Thomas Mann, director of political studies at the Brookings Institution, goes so far as to say "any referendum on any form of direct democracy will pass. A [vote for a] national primary would pass right now [in the United States], and would have passed 20 years ago."[1] In the modern world, the vast majority of political regimes must claim some, if not all, of their legitimacy from the people. It used to be that authority was claimed on the basis of divination from the gods, and most recently, from the authority derived from one God. The kings of France would claim to be able to trace their lineage back to God himself and in this way claim the right to rule over man. Though regimes are often built by force, force is not usually the justification given. Modernity recognized the significance of the individual apart from the group, and in doing so, began to recognize individual rights and liberties. If man could commune with God without a mediator, such as a priest, he could also rule himself without a king. In this way kings and emperors began to lose the sole claim to sovereignty. Thus in today's world, almost every regime, whether it be democratic or authoritarian, must claim some legitimacy from the people (Bendix 1978).

In the Western liberal democratic tradition, the need for legitimacy to come from the people is even greater. In regimes based upon these ideas, the "people" hold sovereignty over the state and thus the state must be legitimized by them. Even in constitutional democracies, the constitutions themselves at least rhetorically depend upon the justification of the people. Few regimes in the twentieth century have escaped this rhetoric, including communist regimes. Though Marx believed that the people at large could not lead themselves to salvation, the elite or vanguard would do so on their behalf.[2]

The Post-Soviet regimes have been, as has been demonstrated throughout this book, no exception to this trend. They have turned to democracy and the "people" to give legitimacy to their regimes. Open and free elections have become the norm, though institutionalization of the rule of law has been a slow process. Executives and legislatures have been partially modeled on France, Britain, and/or the United States in an attempt to adopt entire Western democratic traditions. This process has been mandated because of the fall of Communism and the role it had played in legitimizing a decaying regime and society. The Soviet regime nearly destroyed all traces not only of democracy but also of the church in the social and political affairs of the Central and East European states. Communism and the Party became the official source of all authority and legitimacy. With the delegitimization of Communism, leaders have attempted to substitute democracy with varying results. In fact, Aleksandr Solzhenitsyn has argued not simply for democracy but direct democracy on the local level with national politicians playing a lesser role (Solzhenitsyn 1991).[3]

Post-Soviet regimes have also felt pressure from external, international forces to adopt the institutions and practices of democracy in order to receive economic aid for their transition from command economies. Though the impact of the International Monetary Fund (IMF) and the World Bank can be over-emphasized, their influential role in shaping the economic and political reforms of these states cannot be denied. Inherent in their policies is the theory that economic liberalization depends upon and goes hand-in-hand with political liberalization. Thus, the IMF and World Bank are more likely to lend their support, usually on tacit behalf of the United States, if a regime has adopted a democratic regime (Król 1996; Huntington 1996).

Though the intentions behind using the referendum vary, its ability to be manipulated has been a consistent factor in its popularity. Some leaders use the referendum because it gives the impression of democracy at work without purely democratic results. Others use the referendum as a way to subvert the power of their opponents; the most common example being of executives trying to get around a legislature. Others become fond of the referendum because they see it as a way to link themselves directly with the people; they seek the popular legitimacy and public support that the referendum provides. Some leaders have simply been careless, arrogant, or both in their use of the referendum, which has cost a few their positions.

The Pros and Cons of Referendums

Referendums are Very Susceptible to Manipulation

The ability of leaders to take advantage of the referendum process is one of the chief reasons, if not the chief reason, why referendums are so popular among elites. One of the most significant characteristics of direct democracy in general and the referendum device in specific is the fact that many technical and administrative issues must be decided by someone before the people have a chance to vote. No matter how much care is used, a small group of people, even one single individual, may decide some of the most important aspects of a vote. In the end, the people administering a vote have a great deal of power.

With regard to referendums, the government officials in charge of the referendum have even greater power. If a referendum is constitutionally mandated, then leaders do not have the ability to decide whether or not it will be called, its subject, and probably not even its timing. If a referendum is not constitutionally mandated, then a leader or leaders always choose the referendum subject, timing, and whether or not it is called. Even initiatives, which technically are proposed through the petitioning of government by the people, are usually organized and funded by wealthy and motivated elites often with ties to the current government (Lee 1978, 96–7). Therefore the question of whether or not the people *themselves* have actually chosen to go forward with an initiative becomes suspect. Typically in the case of a referendum, a leader or leaders will decide the subject, whether or not it is called, the wording of the ballot question, the timing of the vote, and the interpretation of the results. Any one of these actions alone can be critical to a referendum's success for a leader; having control over all of them can be the easiest way to orchestrate a desired policy change or law.

Nevertheless, referendum campaigns often go wrong. Gorbachev could not consolidate his 1991 USSR referendum victory. Yeltsin's opponents in the 1993 April Russian referendums attempted to embarrass him with questions on confidence in him and his economic policies, and yet Yeltsin prevailed among the electorate. However, Yeltsin's victory could also not be consolidated until after engaging in armed conflict with Parliament in October. De Gaulle resigned and Pinochet stepped down as president after referendum losses.

Usually executives—presidents, prime ministers, or dictators—have the sole power of deciding a referendum subject and whether or not it is called. If a legislature must vote to allow a referendum to take place it may sometimes have the power to change the wording of a question or add its own questions per the example of Yeltsin and the Russian legislature in the spring of 1993. Some governments allow for the calling of a referendum and its subject to originate in the legislature or by a substantial number of petitioning citizens; this was the case for the Russian government in 1992 and 1993. However, the new Russian Constitution of December 1993 gave the president the sole power to call referendums and decide their subject. In France, the prime minister and not the president could propose a referendum, but the prime minister usually did so on behalf of the president anyway. Though the "two Assemblies" of the French Parliament could also propose a referendum, the Parliament never did so during Charles de Gaulle's tenure as president. Only the French president was empowered finally to call, implement, and enforce a referendum (Constitution of the French Fifth Republic, article 11; Frears 1977, 238). Mikhail Gorbachev, as general secretary of the Communist Party, was a *de facto* autocrat of the Soviet state. Technically, the December 1990 Soviet law on referendums invested the power to hold a referendum in the Congress of People's Deputies or the Supreme Soviet but the lead of the general secretary in all affairs, including the referendum, was usually followed.

The leaders of the Soviet Union, Russia, France, and Chile in the latter part of the twentieth century mostly used direct, popular votes to increase the power of the executive even though many used them in the name of reform. Boris Yeltsin held six constitutional referendums—five dealing with the distribution of power between the executive and legislature in Russia and one dealing with the distribution of power between the Soviet center and Russia. Charles de Gaulle held three constitutional referendums concerning the distribution of power between the executive and legislature and two autonomy referendums dealing with Algeria. Augusto Pinochet held two constitutional referendums and one policy referendum. Mikhail Gorbachev held one autonomy referendum concerning the affirmation of the union of Soviet republics and subsequently the status of the individual republics as a part of it. Three out of four of these leaders had more constitutional referendums than autonomy or policy. Only two out of four leaders had autonomy referendums; the same number had policy referendums. Overall, there were ten constitutional referendums, three autonomy referendums, and two policy referendums. Therefore it is easy to argue that these leaders called a preponderance of referendums on subjects that directly affected their power as executives.

With respect to manipulation, the wording of a referendum question can greatly affect the outcome of the vote and its interpretation afterwards. In April 1993, the Russian legislature added a question to the ballot on the Yeltsin government's economic policies specifically to embarrass Yeltsin. Gorbachev, however, provides the best example of this kind of manipulation with his question in the Soviet referendum on the union treaty. The question read: "Do you consider necessary the preservation of the Union of Soviet Socialist Republics as a renewed federation of equal sovereign republics, in which the rights and freedoms of an individual of any nationality will be fully guaranteed?" Because the question actually contained several questions, no one could really answer it fairly with a simple "Yes" or "No." How could one "preserve" something that was not yet "renewed"? The question assumed that the union that survived would be "socialist" and not just a unified state. Moreover, one could only vote for an alternative union by voting for the total disintegration of the present one.[4] An affirmative answer could be interpreted to mean support for local soviets as a form of state power to the government's use of harsh measures to resolve interethnic tensions.[5] Moreover, no one really knew what the final clause on "equal rights" meant at all. These criticisms led a group of academics to argue that the wording itself violated the referendum law since it was not "clear and neutral" in meaning. The referendum, they concluded, was "politically undesirable, juridically inaccurate, and sociologically unprofessional" and they urged its cancellation.[6] The central Soviet authorities, however, dismissed these objections.

Theoretically, the wording of a referendum question can be manipulated to appeal to the greatest number of voters while retaining the desired outcome. We assumed that voter preferences could be mapped along a single dimension on a particular political issue; this process has been highlighted throughout the study with spatial models. A leader can word a question in such a way that appeals to a majority of the population by simply understanding, either explicitly or intuitively, what the people want to hear. Furthermore we could assume that voters have sets of preferences over other issues or cleavages that might allow leaders adept at wording the opportunity to bring in more voters by referencing certain politically charged symbols or words. Often these crosscutting cleavages may be associated with ethnic, religious, or regional groups. Crosscutting cleavages may also represent a certain public sentiment that the people are well known to have. For example, de Gaulle played upon the French sentiments, expressed in public opinion polls, for stable executive leadership by threatening to resign and upon the French desire to have a directly elected president (Frears 1991, 214). The Russian Parliament added a question on Yeltsin's economic policy because they knew it was unpopular—their hopes were that the public would associate this negativity directly with Yeltsin and approve one of the following ballot questions calling for the early election of the president.

Similarly, the timing of a question can be very important. Leaders may want to call a referendum at the height of their popularity or after the urgency of an event. Sometimes leaders must call a referendum because of a constitutional mandate even though they might rather postpone the vote. Pinochet had to call a referendum on the continuation of his presidency/dictatorship after his 1980 Constitution called for the approval of a candidate from the junta after eight years in office. Yeltsin held a referendum on the establishment of a Russian presidency on the same day and ballot as the all-union referendum in the USSR. Yeltsin also held a Russian referendum in December 1993 on a new constitution, which gave him overwhelming institutional power concentrated in the presidency after the disbandment and shelling of the Parliament in October. De Gaulle held his referendum on the direct election of the president right after the extremely popular settlement of the Algerian crisis and the thought-provoking assassination attempt on his life at Petit Clamart (Frears 1991, 15–16, 214).

The interpretation of referendum results can easily make or break a referendum campaign for an executive; however, an executive usually has a more charismatic appeal to the citizenry and a better platform from which to speak to the public. The most essential question that the initiator of a referendum must answer is what portion of the citizenry grants legitimacy: the majority of the electorate or the majority of those voting. A vaguely worded question, such as Gorbachev's on the union treaty, can be interpreted to give legitimacy to anything the referendum question can be twisted to support. For example, the language in Gorbachev's that reads " ... the rights and freedoms of an individual of any nationality will be fully guaranteed," can be interpreted to mean that the Soviet Union has the right to intervene in republic or local affairs in order to "guarantee" the "rights and freedoms of an individual or any nationality." Many observers inside and outside of the USSR took this to mean that the Soviet Union could intervene with force, like in the case of Lithuania in January 1991, in order to protect a Russian "minority."[7]

Even if the referendum accurately captures the public will, a majority of the people may still be manipulated by a leader; majorities, in short, do not always make the best decisions. While some arguments against direct democracy may be considered elitist and paternalistic, others are grounded in the observation that large groups of people can become susceptible to manipulation through emotion, populism, and extremism. Minority concerns can become completely overwhelmed with a referendum. Even in the case of the election of a candidate using a majoritarian voting system, the candidate still may reach out and seek some kind of compromise. Referendums, on the other hand, provide no flexibility for change over time.

Thus there has been a troubling use of the referendum device against ethnic, religious, and other minority concerns. In the former Soviet Union, there have been numerous referendums featuring ethnic or religious minorities. While Estonia approved a measure allowing noncitizens to vote in 1992, two referendums have been proposed but never called in Lithuania to restrict the rights of foreigners and noncitizens. Georgia held a referendum for its citizens who were refugees from the Abkhazia region in 1996 that denounced legislative elections held there on November 23. In the Russian region of Kabardino-Balkariya, the ethnic Balkars voted amongst themselves only to join the Russian Federation in 1991 as a separate entity but later decided against it. The Russian-speaking majority within the Crimean region of the Ukraine has proposed at least ten referendums and held several calling at a minimum for some autonomy and at most for secession from the Ukraine. Russian-speaking majorities in the Donetsk and Lugansk regions of the Ukraine have held referendums similar to those in the Crimea.

Referendums and the Public Will

The ability of referendums to measure the public will depends upon the premise that the public will can be effectively measured by the referendum device. Consider that a referendum is very similar to a public opinion poll except for the fact that public opinion polling is done much more carefully. Public opinion polling has become a very sophisticated enterprise in which much time, skill, and money is used to form an accurate portrayal of the public will. Painstaking effort is taken to insure that the respondents are representative of the population as a whole. Moreover, many questions are asked, not just one, in order to understand the nuances of the public's attitude toward a subject. It is well understood that the public will is not only complex but sometimes unexplainable with regards to rationality: the creation of the public will from the collection of many individual preferences and preference orders sometimes proves incoherent (Ordeshook 1986).[8]

Referendum voting provides a particularly difficult case for divining the public will. Only one question is usually asked per measure; moreover, the public is asked to vote yes or no on the question. The public does not have a choice over other options. If the question includes wording that voters do not like, then they must decide whether or not it is worth voting down the whole measure. Therefore, the wording of a question can include language that directs the voters to vote one way or another.

Many political theorists believe institutions of representative democracy do a better job of expressing the people's will than the referendum and other institutions of direct democracy. Leaders like referendums because they grant legitimacy to their goals by nominally expressing the people's will; however, there are several ways to express the people's will in governance. The referendum is a device of direct democracy along with the initiative and recall vote. These devices are usually contrasted with the institutions of representative democracy: the legislature, the executive, and the courts. The supporters and detractors of direct democracy are not confined to any particular ideological perspective or historical time period. Among political theorists, Jean Jacques Rousseau, Karl Marx, and Friedrich Engels have argued that direct democracy was preferable to representative democracy. In particular, supporters of direct democracy have argued against elites and elitism. Referendums therefore serve as an effective way to insert the people's will into the decision-making process in order to make it less elitist. In the United States, the Progressive movement at the turn of the twentieth century and neo-conservatives since World War II have all argued for the use of the referendum as a means by which to blunt elitism (Held 1996; Butler and Ranney 1978).

Many prominent scholars and practitioners, on the other hand, have criticized direct democracy, including Plato, Aristotle, Hobbes, John Stuart Mill, James Madison, Alexander Hamilton, Max Weber, and William H. Riker (1982). John Stuart Mill has argued that institutions of direct democracy like the referendum work best in small communities (Mill 1951). Noteworthy examples include the Athenian City-State (or Republic), New England town meetings, frontier town meetings in the westward expansion across the United States, and communist cells or soviets. Nevertheless, even these examples have their caveats. In Ancient Athens, only Athenian males over 20 years of age could participate in governance while women, foreigners, and slaves were excluded. In fact it has been argued that the only reason Athenian males had the time and energy to participate in direct democracy was because of slavery and the subservient role of women in their society (Held 1996). Communist cells and soviets could work democratically as long as they remained small. Once they became large they added the tenet of *democratic centralism* and other nondemocratic changes in order to make their meetings and decisions more efficient. The American town meetings were always very small affairs.

Referendums have an extensive track record in only a few countries.[9] The referendum device is not usually part of a comprehensive system of direct democracy but a part of a federal, representative democracy. The only country that has put the referendum to anything but occasional use is Switzerland. Referendums in Switzerland are always mandatory—their results must always be implemented. Constitutional revisions and amendments made by the central government are compulsory and must be called. Citizens may also call a referendum to revise the constitution after collecting 100,000 signatures. Referendums on laws and decrees passed by the legislature are optional. Only citizens may petition and demand that a referendum be called on a law or decree passed by the legislature; they must petition ninety days within publication of the law or decree and collect 50,000 signatures. However, no central authority—an executive, legislature, or government—can call an optional referendum (Aubert 1978).

Referendums and Conflict

Of all the characteristics and effects associated with referendums, its ability, or inability, to formulate a compromise between competing leaders, elites, and groups is the most politically volatile. The institutions of representative democracy—chief among them the legislature—require that participants compromise their position on an issue in order to develop a consensus that can be supported by enough legislators for passage. Legislators follow a process of considering the issues, hearing the arguments, receiving recommendations from committees and experts, and engaging in debate. It takes time and sustained interest on the part of the legislators to make laws. Moreover, there is further incentive to compromise because a law can be passed much quicker if a consensus can be reached. However, institutions of representative democracy may also repress the ideas and welfare of minority concerns and groups; this repression may lead, eventually, to violent conflict.

Referendums do not have to follow any kind of formal process in which debate, expert advice, and thoughtful consideration are involved. Because every citizen belongs to the debate, it is impossible to get everyone in one forum to discuss an issue, but more importantly, one would not want to. Therefore, referendum campaigns become like election campaigns except there are no candidate debates because there are no candidates. Moreover, anything can be said by anyone on behalf of an issue, but the campaigns with the most organization and money have a clear advantage (Broder 2000).

Referendum questions set up an all-or-nothing, winner-takes-all situation when the stakes are high and potential for redress is low; circumstances that are often found in transitional politics.[10] In game theoretic terms, the situation can be described as zero-sum: a referendum proponent's gain is the opponent's loss. An issue decided by referendum often leaves an issue's opponents unsatisfied and sometimes unwilling to comply. The empirical record established by this work's Large-N Data Set analysis of Soviet and Post-Soviet referendums does not statistically support the hypothesis that violence results from calling a referendum, but an anecdotal argument based on the case studies presented can be made for the referendum device playing an intermediate role. In other words, referendums do not seem to cause violence but they may reveal it and play a role in increasing tensions between referendum participants that can affect decisions concerning the use of force.

Sometimes referendums have played a useful role in revealing tensions and resolving potential violent conflict. The French votes on Algerian independence are the best example of how referendums can resolve a dangerous situation. In the beginning, the French military and polity was divided and unsure of how to deal with Algeria and its push for independence; this problem was one of the chief reasons Charles de Gaulle was brought back into government in the late 1950s. De Gaulle adeptly maneuvered between both military and political factions toward an end that a majority of the French people desired. In doing so, he successfully used the referendum device to insert the will of the people into the debate on Algeria. The first referendum in January 1961 made clear the French people's view that Algeria had a right to seek its independence. The second vote in April 1962 cemented the legitimacy of de Gaulle's negotiated peace settlement with Algeria that assured its independence.

In the Soviet and Post-Soviet states, referendums have been specifically utilized after attempts to reach a compromise by political actors on various issues had failed. For example, Yeltsin failed to reach a compromise with his political opponents in the Congress of People's Deputies and Supreme Soviet on details of an economic program for Russia; thus, he turned to the referendum as a way out of deadlock. In the Post-Soviet states in general, the referendum was a way out of deadlock that included a better than even chance of winning and achieving one's goals. De Gaulle and Pinochet, however, called their referendums less out of desperation and more out of calculation. De Gaulle did not discuss with Parliament the idea of directly electing the president or of devolving power away from the Senate before proposing those votes. Likewise, Pinochet planned for the referendum device to be a part of his grand scheme of holding power; he never planned a referendum as a way to resolve policy deadlock. Gorbachev thought that his proposed use of the referendum device was a smart tactical move in the face of opposition from the republics (Matlock 1995, 476).

Gorbachev's policy dilemma centered upon the ratification of a new union treaty that would define the relationship of the center to the republics. He not only faced the opposition of various republics within the USSR—chief among them the Baltic states with their desire to secede—but he also faced the reticence of the Communist old guard and apparat, which preferred to crack down on independence movements than give them any audience. None of the republics liked Gorbachev's draft of the new union treaty he made public in November 1990; they all deemed it to be restrictive and demanded amendments. Gorbachev, instead of compromising, decided at the fourth Congress of People's Deputies to propose a referendum on the new draft treaty. Instead of fostering compromise, the referendum spawned a host of counter-referendums, boycotts, and republic-level changes to the question. Before the referendum had even taken place, Estonia, Latvia, and Lithuania had already held successful independence referendums— a Georgian independence vote followed soon after the all-union vote. Kirghizia, Uzbekistan, and the Ukraine added a question to the all-union referendum calling for status as "equal sovereign republics." This referendum victory gave strength to the conservative and hard-line opposition while doing nothing to resolve the matter for the republics that desired more autonomy.

Afterward, Gorbachev did attempt to negotiate with the republics and draft a compromise union treaty that would give them some autonomy, but his compromises drew the ire of conservatives and hard-liners, and eventually led to a failed coup d'état staged by them. Had Gorbachev sought compromise in the beginning it is possible that conservatives and hard-liners in the central government along with the independence-minded reformers in the republics could have agreed upon a union treaty acceptable to them both. Instead, the referendum may have forced them to harden their positions because it affirmed their belief that a majority of Soviet citizens wanted the union preserved. What the referendum did do was increase the tension in society between its constituent parts. As the Staff of the Commission on Security and Cooperation in Europe reports, "It laid bare the conflicts between center and republics, between republics and their constituent parts, between different nationalities inhabiting those regions and between political movements already inclined to view their differences in Manichean terms" (Staff of the Commission on Security and Cooperation in Europe 1991).

Though Yeltsin's opponents in the legislature allowed a modified set of referendum questions to be presented to the public in the spring of 1993 on economic reform and early elections for Parliament, they never agreed afterward to support the results. The policy deadlock between Yeltsin and the Parliament from the winter of 1992 through the spring of 1993 culminated in a series of arguments and threats until the Parliament decided to go ahead with the referendum albeit with questions they had modified. Included in this list of questions was one designed specifically to embarrass Yeltsin: "Do you approve the socio-economic policies implemented by the President of the Russian Federation and the government of the Russian Federation since 1992?" Nevertheless, Yeltsin won all four of these votes and fully expected to be able to carry out his policies.

However, Ruslan Khasbulatov—Chairman of the Supreme Soviet—and other key hard-liners thwarted every attempt by Yeltsin to capitalize on his referendum victory. Khasbulatov blocked Yeltsin's effort to adopt a new constitution by returning to his old argument that the current document should be amended gradually one piece at a time, and he resisted Yeltsin's call for new, multiparty elections for Parliament in the fall of 1993. Inevitably, tensions began to rise between the president and Parliament (McAuley 1997, 41). Under Khasbulatov's guidance in the summer of 1993, the Supreme Soviet sought to thwart the tight budget restraints and voucher privatization program of the Yeltsin government's economic policy (Brudny 1995, 93). Moreover Khasbulatov planned to submit constitutional amendments to the Congress of People's Deputies that would remove Yeltsin as head of the Security Council and take away his ability to sign international treaties (Brudny 1995, 94). It seemed as if Khasbulatov was attempting to bait President Yeltsin into a showdown that Khasbulatov believed he could win (Brudny 1995, 94).

In his most famous referendums, Charles de Gaulle went straight to the people with his concerns and did not negotiate beforehand with his political enemies. As de Gaulle's tenure in office stretched through the 1960s, he sought to bypass Parliament more and more. In this way, de Gaulle used the referendum not simply as a tool but as a weapon in the eyes of his parliamentary enemies. In 1962 he proposed a referendum for the direct election of the president instead of by the current system of an electoral college made up of councilors and deputies. In 1969 he proposed a referendum that would strengthen regional councils by devolving power away from the Senate—the Senate, of course, being the actual target of the referendum. As the decade proceeded, de Gaulle increasingly desired to face opposition not by negotiation but by direct appeal to the people of France. In doing so he would always threaten to resign if the people did not support his policies. This "my way or the highway" philosophy infuriated his political opponents and his use of the referendum device eventually inflamed a political conflict so great that on losing his 1969 referendum he resigned.

Chile presents an interesting referendum case involving President Salvador Allende and the coup d'état that overthrew him. The story begins in the last days of the Allende regime when it seemed as if the political stalemate between Allende's party Unidad Popular (UP) and the Center-Right and far Right would end in violence. The parliamentary elections of March 1973 did not resolve the conflict over the socialization of the economy embodied in the UP's economic program *Área de propiedad social* (APS). Society had become polarized around the issue in the first three years of the Allende regime with opposition growing even at the grass roots level. After an attempt at compromise failed with the PDC, Allende came to the conclusion that a referendum was the last best chance to resolve the stalemate in his favor.

It seems as if the referendum, irrespective of the formal subject, would in effect decide both Allende's tenure and his policies (Davis 1985, 217). Though he did not yet have the support of the Socialist Party, he went ahead with plans to announce the referendum publicly on September 11. Allende informed Generals Pinochet and Urbina on September 9 that he would call a referendum "so that the country may decide which way to go"; the generals were astonished on hearing the news (Garcés 1974, 353). The day of the scheduled referendum announcement was the day the coup took place; it had begun early in the morning long before Allende was able to arrive at the presidential palace to make his scheduled noon speech announcing the vote.

Though the referendum proposal was certainly not the cause of the coup, it may be argued that the referendum proposal was the proximate cause, or trigger, of the Chilean coup d'état. Originally the coup had been set for September 14, but Pinochet stated afterward that the decision to move the coup up to September 11 had been made on the afternoon of September 9—the day he learned from Allende of the upcoming September 11 referendum announcement (Pinochet 1980, 120–3). The military junta decided to begin the coup on the day Allende was to announce the referendum; thus, the referendum proposal may have "hastened the coup" (Oppenheim 1993, 85; Kaufman 1988, 295–6). Though tensions were at a crisis level by August 1973 without the referendum, the upcoming referendum proposal may have been the last justification needed to carry out the coup. This series of events certainly demonstrates the power of the referendum because it created fear in the hearts of the military junta. The power of the referendum device lay in its legitimacy and legitimating power.

Referendums and the Laws they Make

The sponsor of a referendum often wants the wording of a question to be vague in order to garner as many votes as possible, but if the referendum is passed, the same question usually makes bad law. Even if the referendum question is clear, what usually matters most for a law is how it is implemented and the regulations developed to guide its implementation. Regulations, however, cannot be voted on or attached to a referendum ballot; they are usually written by the legislature in committee with the help of experts. For political reasons, a referendum sponsor may wish to interpret a referendum question differently after the vote has been taken, which may lead to further confusion.

Another problem arises over the precedence of a successful referendum over current and future laws. Unless it is explicitly stated in a referendum law or constitution, what overrides a referendum can be very difficult to ascertain. A referendum will usually take precedence over a legislated law. It is unclear what happens if a law is relegislated that has been decided by referendum. The Soviet law on referendums and the Russian law on referendums from 1992 to 1993 stated that a referendum could only be overturned by another referendum; referendums carried "supreme legal force" (White et al. 1997, 73). In the United States, referendums have been found unconstitutional by the judiciary. Judicial review in countries that are transitioning to or consolidating democracy might not carry the same force.

Finally, referendums sometimes create laws in a politically contentious environment that may result in problematic implementation. Referendum opponents can be angry and resentful, and may even proclaim the vote and/or the process illegitimate. As an institution of direct democracy, the referendum device can raise tensions between opposing positions. In some cases referendum opponents may attempt to block the implementation of the referendum. Opponents in the executive or legislature are ideally positioned to block a referendum's implementation. Likewise, ordinary citizens, elites, and leaders within institutions can appeal to the judiciary to strike down a referendum for being unconstitutional; it is also possible to attack a referendum as being impossible to implement. The ideal example of this occurred after Yeltsin won the referendums of April 1993. The legislature, led by Ruslan Khasbulatov, stymied the implementation of the measures drawn up by Yeltsin in light of his victory at the polls. In the end, the policy and constitutional disputes between Yeltsin and the Russian legislature were decided by force in favor of Yeltsin.

The Virtue and Vice of Referendum Politics

This study has shown that executives, along with other political actors, can use referendums effectively to achieve their goals through the expression of the will of the people. This device is an important tool for the executive, and others, because it grants legitimacy to and can change the distribution of power between individuals, groups, institutions, and even autonomous and semiautonomous state structures. All types of referendums—autonomy, constitutional, and policy—may all be manipulated either for the good or ill of the public at large.

Referendums play a crucial and distinct role in transitions. Periods of state transition and consolidation increase the importance and potential abuse of the referendum device because bargaining between elites involves high stakes coupled with a fluid nature of power. The critical distinction during fluid political times with respect to referendums is whether these votes legitimize institutional change as opposed to policy change. While policy changes may be critical to a state's transition, referendums that change the distribution of power between institutions, or state and federal structures, may determine a country's political fortunes for decades. In transition times as opposed to times of stability, there will be more referendums concerning constitutional and autonomy issues because power is up for grabs.

Leaders, particularly those in executive positions of power, will continue to be attracted to these devices. Referendums, simple in use but complex in effect, challenge legislative institutions by directly connecting the people to the executive. But even legislatures understand the utility in using a direct popular vote when other means of achieving a goal have been exhausted. Overall, because the referendum device has the ability to grant political legitimacy and power and to connect leaders with the people, this institution will continue to play a role in politics—for good and for ill.

Notes

Chapter 1　Legitimacy, Bargaining, and Power in the Use of Referendums

1. I have chosen to use the English plural *referendums* instead of the Latin plural *referenda*.
2. I do not draw a distinction between the term *referendum* and the term *plebiscite*. Many distinguish plebiscites from referendums by their use; plebiscites are seen as being undemocratic because of misuse or manipulation. Some would describe a plebiscite as a populist use of a referendum. The examples of referendum use by Napoleon and Hitler are often given. However, in my opinion, there is no valid intellectual or conceptual distinction between the two terms.
3. Even constitutions are not considered legitimate unless the people vote for them either directly or through their representatives. In fact it is becoming more the norm that people vote for constitutions directly as demonstrated by the adoption of constitutions in the Post-Soviet states by referendum.
4. In transitions from Communism, political institutions are often weak in the absolute sense of being able unilaterally to make policy and in the relative sense of being of comparable power with other political institutions. While I have executives and legislature mostly in mind with regards to the latter, the same also applies to federal and regional political structures.
5. The Median Voter Theorem argues that the position of the median voter can defeat any alternative over a single issue in a pairwise vote (Morrow 1994, 104).
6. Describing the political spectrum of a group of countries that includes former Communist states can be difficult because the Western notions of the political "left," "right," "conservative," and "liberal" do not make sense in the Soviet and Post-Soviet experience. The best way to capture politics inclusive of these regions posits a spectrum that goes from "Liberal" and "Non-Communist" to "Non-Liberal" and "Communist."

7. These categories have been designed so that it makes sense to progress linearly from one concept to the next. Thus, these are radial categories as opposed to classical categories (Lakoff 1987).
8. The Post-Soviet states include Estonia, Latvia, Lithuania, Russia, Belarus, the Ukraine, Moldova, Georgia, Armenia, Azerbaijan, Kazakhstan, Uzbekistan, Tajikistan, Turkmenistan, and Kyrgyzstan.
9. Theoretically, referendums can change the distribution of power between institutions in non-transition times but this is rare. Times of transition provide an opportunity for great change to take place in society and its institutions because change is often seen as being needed. Times of stability, on the other hand, do not require change to take place; usually change is avoided in an attempt to preserve stability. On a cognitive level, most individuals are simply not open to change in a noncrisis, non-transition atmosphere. Moreover, if a people are on the verge of changing their society's institutional make-up then they are essentially entering into a transition phase.
10. This is similar to McFaul's definition of state power (1995). McFaul posits that the state is a set of government institutions that define and implement national policy.
11. The Baltic republics—Estonia, Latvia, and Lithuania—held independence votes before the March 17, 1991 all-Union referendum. Russia, Kyrgyzstan, and the Ukraine held votes important to their sovereignty on the same day as the all-Union referendum while Georgia held a similar vote immediately afterwards.
12. Initiatives are proposed by the public or a citizen group. Some treat initiatives as a subcategory of referendums while others see initiatives as being a separate institution and define referendums as votes originating from the government. Because I believe that initiatives can be manipulated by elites as well as referendums, I do not draw such a stark line between the two.

Chapter 2   Referendums and Executives in France and Chile

1. Cited in John R. Frears, 1977, *Political Parties and Elections in the French Fifth Republic*, New York: St. Martin's Press, 239. Original citation: " 'Le plébiscite, ça ne se dispute pas, ça se bat,' Radio interview."
2. "I am the state."
3. In this case de Gaulle's threat to resign from office was not perceived by the voters as a decisive negative weight on the reversion point. In other words, the French people would rather see de Gaulle resign than allow the referendum to pass.
4. Though Pinochet did step down as president, he remained in command of the military forces.

5. Roger Cohen, "Voted Out: Rejecting Pinochet, Chile Faces a Period of Promise and Peril; Economy Thrives but Needs Stability, and that May be Scarce for Many Months," *Wall-Street-Journal*, 212: 1 O 7 1988.

6. See Jack Hayward, 1969, "Presidential Suicide by Plebiscite: De Gaulle's Exit," *Parliamentary Affairs* 22: 289. His use of the word "plebiscite" implies that he believed the vote was designed "to provide passive support for a leader and confirm the legitimacy of his authority" and not as a means for the voters "to express their specific demands upon the political system."

7. Frears, *Political Parties and Elections in the French Fifth Republic*, 239.

8. Jack Hayward, 1969, "Presidential Suicide by Plebiscite: De Gaulle's Exit," *Parliamentary Affairs* 22: 289.

9. *Plebiscite* is a much older word than *referendum*. *Plebiscite* derives from the vote of the plebs in Rome in the fourth century B.C. and was the term used in France in the eighteenth and nineteenth centuries. The word *referendum* came into use in English in the 1880s though Swiss cantons referred to actions as *ad referendum* two centuries earlier (Butler and Ranney 1978, 4).

10. On June 14, 1946 de Gaulle gave a speech at Bayeux describing the "institutions that France needs" (Lacouture 1991, 193).

11. Serge Berstein, 1993, *The Republic of de Gaulle, 1958–1969*, New York: Cambridge University Press, 9.

12. Charismatic authority is a term from Max Weber's *Theory of Social and Economic Organization*. Charismatic authority is defined as the title to rule based on "devotion to the specific and exceptional sanctity, heroism or exemplary character of an individual person."

13. There is some controversy over whether Pompidou was "fired" or if he "resigned." Though Pompidou had asked de Gaulle several times during the preceding week to accept his resignation, de Gaulle only did so after Pompidou had departed on Friday, July 5. Pompidou had been wavering in the face of the opposition of his friends and colleagues to his resignation, and had, in fact, decided to stay on that night. Too late, however, since it seems as if de Gaulle had finally decided to let him go that night also. Pompidou heard that de Gaulle had accepted his resignation the next day.

14. Charles de Gaulle, 1970, *Discours et Messages*, Paris: Plon, V, 407. Quoted in Jean Lacouture, 1991, *De Gaulle: The Ruler 1945–1970*, New York: W. W. Norton & Company, 575.

15. It is not clear whether Allende would have won the referendum he was planning to call. Winning a referendum vote would have depended greatly upon the actual question he asked and its timing with other events or elections. However it is certainly possible that Allende could have shrewdly crafted a question and timed it such that he could have maximized the vote in his favor.

16. Roger Cohen, "Voted out."

17. Ibid.

18. Ibid.

19. As reported to me by a "consultant" to Pinochet on the referendum who was present for at least part of the campaign. Supposedly the air force and navy

commanders were against canceling the referendum results because they did not wish to antagonize the international community and possibly lose their source of high technology weapons and systems for their forces.

20. Cohen, "Voted out."

Chapter 3   The USSR Referendum and Republic Counter-Referendums

1. Estonia held five referendums between 1923 and 1936 while Latvia held one referendum in 1931. Lithuania held its first referendum in 1991. The countries of Eastern Europe also held referendums beginning in 1920 but they are beyond the scope of this study.

2. There is a difference between republic sovereignty and independence. Sovereignty declarations and referendums seemed to suggest that a republic wanted more say over their dealings but did not necessarily want to secede; sovereignty desires probably equate best with the level of independence found in a confederation of states. Republic independence is about secession.

3. M. S. Gorbachev, "Gorbachev Airs Personal Feelings on Reform," *Current Digest of the Soviet Press*, XLII, No. 48 (Jan. 2, 1991): 2. "Speech by M. S. Gorbachev [at a meeting with cultural leaders in the Kremlin on Nov. 28]. (*Pravda and Izvestia*, Dec. 1, 1990, p. 4. 4,500 words. Condensed text.)"

4. Ibid., pp. 2–3.

5. Ibid., p. 9.

6. Ibid., p. 108.

7. As noted earlier, there is a difference between republic sovereignty and independence. Sovereignty desires probably equate best with the level of independence found in a confederation of states. Republic independence is about secession.

8. *Izvestia*, Jan. 18, p. 3; *Current Digest of the Soviet Press*, 43, No. 3: p. 29; FBIS DR, Jan. 17, 1991, p. 17.

9. See the interview with Nursultan Nazarbaev of Kazakhstan in FBIS DR Supplement, Mar. 20, 1991, p. 72.

10. FBIS DR, Feb. 15, 1991, pp. 36–7.

11. Alexander, Rubtsov, *Moscow News*, No. 9.

12. FBIS DR, Feb. 20, 1991, p. 56.

13. FBIS DR, Feb. 15, 1991, p. 36–7.

14. Though it is true that the French 1961 and April 1962 referendums dealing with Algeria did involve subregional politics, the politics of France and Algeria showed none of the forementioned complications. The referendum device did not spawn counter-, or "dueling," referendums. Moreover, the majority of people within both Algeria and France were united in their agreement that Algeria should be allowed its freedom. In fact most departments of Algeria supported independence; only the European-dominated Algiers City voted against Algerian independence in the 1961

vote. In July 1962, 99.72% of the electorate—Muslim and European—voted in favor of the country's independence in their own internal referendum (Berstein 1993).

15. See the interview with Nazarbaev in FBIS DR Supplement, Mar. 20, 1991, p. 72.
16. *Izvestiya*, Mar. 28, 1991: 1, 3. See also White et al. 1997 and Staff of the Commission on Security and Cooperation in Europe 1991.
17. *Izvestiya*, Mar. 26, 1991: 2. See also White et al. 1997 and Staff of the Commission on Security and Cooperation in Europe 1991.
18. FBIS DR, Apr. 1, 1991, p. 43.
19. This figure is taken from the official results of the Russian 1991 presidential election published by the Central Electoral Committee in *Rossiyskaia gazeta* on June 20, 1991.
20. The nine republics were Russia, the Ukraine, Belarus, Azerbaijan, Kazakhstan, Turkmenistan, Kyrgyzstan, Uzbekistan, and Tadjikistan.

Chapter 4   Bargaining and Power in Russian Referendums

1. *Izvestiya*, Dec. 25, 1990.
2. For a discussion of this see Richard Johnston, Andre Blais, Henry E. Brady, and Jean Crete, *Letting the People Decide: Dynamics of a Canadian Election*, Stanford: Stanford University Press, 1992.
3. In fact, de Gaulle did exactly that. He resigned after he lost the 1968 referendum on the devolution of power away from the federal Senate, home to his political opponents, to regional councils.
4. Moscow ITAR-TASS in English, 1636 GMT, Feb. 19, 1993; FBIS DR, Feb. 22, 1993, p. 29.
5. Moscow *Kuranty* in Russian, Mar. 10, 1993, p. 4; FBIS DR, Mar. 11, 1993, p. 52.
6. Could not find Russian language reference source; FBIS DR, Mar. 12, 1993, p. 3.
7. Moscow *Kuranty* in Russian, Mar. 10, 1993, p. 4; FBIS DR, Mar. 11, 1993, p. 52; FBIS DR, Mar. 12, 1993, p. 3.
8. Moscow *Izvestiya* in Russian, Apr. 10, 1993, first edition, p. 2; FBIS DR, Apr. 12, 1993, pp. 26–7.
9. Rome *L'UNITA* in Italian, Apr. 14, 1993, p. 13; FBIS DR, Apr. 19, 1993, p. 49.
10. Moscow *Izvestiya* in Russian, Apr. 17, 1993, first edition, p. 4; FBIS DR, Apr. 21, 1993, p. 33.
11. Moscow Ostankino Television First Channel and Orbita Networks in Russian 1845 GMT, Apr. 19, 1993; FBIS DR, Apr. 22, 1993, p. 34.
12. Moscow ITAR-TASS in English, 1634 GMT, Apr. 22, 1993; FBIS DR, Apr. 23, 1993, p. 32.

13. Moscow ITAR-TASS, in English, 0803 GMT, Apr. 23, 1993; FBIS DR, Apr. 23, 1993, p. 33.
14. *Rossiiskaya gazeta*, May 6, 1993: 1. See also White et al. 1997 and Staff of the Commission on Security and Cooperation in Europe 1993.
15. Yitzhak M. Brudny, "Ruslan Khasbulatov, Aleksandr Rutskoi, and Intraelite Conflict in Post Communist Russia, 1991–1994," in *Patterns in Post-Soviet Leadership*, ed. Timothy J. Colton and Robert C. Tucker, Oxford: Westview Press, 1995, p. 93.
16. Ibid., p. 93.
17. Ibid., p. 94.
18. Ibid., p. 94.
19. Ruslan Khasbulatov, "Tol'ko v usloviiakh demokratii vozmozhny reformy dlia naroda," *Rossiiskaya gazeta*, Sep. 21, 1993: 3–4.
20. *Rossiiskie vesti*, Dec. 25, 1993: 1. See also White et al. 1997.

Chapter 5   Patterns in the Use of Referendums

1. Lithuania, Latvia, Estonia, Armenia, Moldova, and Georgia boycotted the referendum; Lithuania, Latvia, Estonia, and Georgia held referendums on independence. Russia, the Ukraine, Uzbekistan, and Kyrgyzstan called Gorbachev's question but decided to add a question to the all-Union ballot; the Ukraine, Uzbekistan and Kyrgyzstan added a question on their status as a "equal sovereign republic." Kazakhstan changed the wording of Gorbachev's question. Only Azerbaijan, Belorussia, Tajikistan, and Turkmenistan held the referendum as Gorbachev wanted.
2. FBIS-SOV-94-020, Jan. 31, 1994, p. 62.
3. FBIS-SOV-94-020, Jan. 31, 1994, p. 62.
4. Sherimkulov gave Akayev a positive vote of confidence in the referendum.
5. FBIS-SOV-94-020, Jan. 31, 1994, p. 63.
6. FBIS-SOV-94-020, Jan. 31, 1994, p. 62.
7. FBIS-SOV-94-010, Jan. 14, 1994, p. 85.
8. FBIS-SOV-94-010, Jan. 14, 1994, p. 85.
9. FBIS-SOV-94-025, Feb. 7, 1994, p. 57.
10. FBIS-SOV-94-010, Jan. 14, 1994, p. 85.
11. FBIS-SOV-94-020, Jan. 31, 1994, p. 63.
12. FBIS-SOV-94-020, Jan. 31, 1994, p. 63.
13. FBIS-SOV-94-020, Jan. 31, 1994, p. 63.
14. FBIS-SOV-94-030, Feb. 14, 1994, p. 57.
15. FBIS-SOV-94-030, Feb. 14, 1994, p. 57.
16. FBIS-SOV-94-172, Sep. 6, 1994, p. 88.
17. FBIS-SOV-94-173, Sep. 7, 1994, p. 60.
18. FBIS-SOV-94-181, Sep. 19, 1994, p. 60.

19. In parliamentary systems of governance, the "government" consists of cabinet-level officials: prime minister, minister of defense, foreign minister, etc. Kyrgyzstan, like many other Post-Soviet republics, has a quasi-presidential system in which the leading political parties within Parliament form a "government" side-by-side with the election of a president. The "government" is usually beholden in practice to the president, however. This form of government had its origins in France with de Gaulle in the Fifth Republic.

20. FBIS-SOV-94-181, Sep. 19, 1994, p. 60.

21. FBIS-SOV-94-186, Sep. 26, 1994, pp. 60–1.

22. FBIS-SOV-94-195, Oct. 7, 1994, p. 27.

23. FBIS-SOV-94-195, Oct. 7, 1994, p. 28.

24. FBIS-SOV-94-195, Oct. 7, 1994, p. 27.

25. FBIS-SOV-94-195, Oct. 7, 1994, p. 27.

26. FBIS-SOV-94-195, Oct. 7, 1994, p. 28.

27. FBIS-SOV-94-197, Oct. 12, 1994, p. 50.

28. FBIS-SOV-94-197, Oct. 12, 1994, pp. 50–1.

29. FBIS-SOV-94-197, Oct. 12, 1994, pp. 50–1.

30. FBIS-SOV-94-209, Oct. 28, 1994, p. 28.

31. FBIS-SOV-94-212, Nov. 2, 1994, p. 44.

32. It is worth noting that the Kyrgyz Central Electoral commission was appointed by the president and not elected by Parliament as it had been envisioned by the Constitution. See FBIS-SOV-94-212, Nov. 2, 1994, p. 44.

33. Bruce Pannier, OMRI, Inc., Region: Transcaucasia and Central Asia, 95-04-04.

34. Bruce Pannier, OMRI, Inc., Region: Transcaucasia and Central Asia, 95-09-21.

35. Bruce Pannier, OMRI, Inc., Region: Transcaucasia and Central Asia, 96-01-04.

36. FBIS-SOV-94-005, Jan. 7, 1994, pp. 41–2.

37. FBIS-SOV-94-075, Apr. 19, 1994, p. 52.

38. FBIS-SOV-94-075, Apr. 19, 1994, p. 52.

39. Chrystyna Lapychak, "East-Central Europe Ukrainian President Again Threatens Plebiscite Over Bill on Separation of Powers," OMRI Daily Digest, Region: CIS, 95-05-15.

40. Chrystyna Lapychak, "East-Central Europe Ukrainian Parliament Passes Bill on Separation of Powers," OMRI Daily Digest, Region: CIS, 95-05-19.

41. Chrystyna Lapychak, "East-Central Europe Ukrainian President Issues Another Decree on Referendum," OMRI Daily Digest, Region: Transcaucasia and Central Asia, 95-06-06.

42. Chrystyna Lapychak, "Ukrainian President Insists on Referendum on New Constitution," OMRI Daily Digest, Region: Central and Eastern Europe, 95-11-13.

43. Ibid.

44. Ibid.
45. Roman Solchanyk, "Referendum Campaign in the Crimea," *OMRI Daily Digest*, Region: Successor States to the USSR, 92-02-04.
46. Roman Solchanyk, "Crimean Referendum Campaign," *OMRI Daily Digest*, Region: Successor States to the USSR, 92-04-07.
47. Bohdan Nahaylo, "Kravchuk Warns Against Crimean Referendum," *OMRI Daily Digest*, Region: Successor States to the USSR, 92-04-21.
48. Bohdan Nahaylo, "Kravchuk Warns Against Crimean Referendum," *OMRI Daily Digest*, Region: Successor States to the USSR, 92-04-21.
49. Roman Solchanyk, "Crimea to Remain Part of Ukraine," *OMRI Daily Digest*, Region: Successor States to the USSR, 92-05-07.
50. Roman Solchanyk, "Crimean Referendum Asks Two Questions," *OMRI Daily Digest*, Region: Successor States to the USSR, 92-05-07.
51. Roman Solchanyk, "Ukrainian Parliament Annuls Crimean Independence," *OMRI Daily Digest*, Region: Successor States to the USSR, 92-04-14.
52. Ibid.
53. FBIS-SOV-94-055, Mar. 22, 1994, pp. 38–9.
54. FBIS-SOV-94-062, Mar. 31, 1994, p. 35.
55. Chrystyna Lapychak, "East-Central Europe Ukraine Moves to Limit Crimean Autonomy," *OMRI Daily Digest*, Region: Transcaucasia and Central Asia, 95-03-20.
56. Note that because the referendums observed in the two years of 1990 and 1997 were extremely small in number (5), compared to the six years of 1991 through 1996 (147), they have been omitted in some analyses. Therefore take note that the total number of referendums proposed and/or called in this chapter will change, depending upon the analyses being conducted, from either the 147 referendums from 1991 to 1996 to the 152 referendums from 1990 to 1997.
57. The research for this data includes primary and secondary source material collected in Russian and English, and includes official government reports, newspaper articles, television and radio stories, and academic articles and books. Extensive time was spent in archives in Moscow, Berkeley, Stanford, Washington, D.C., and on the Internet. Special thanks should be given to the Foreign Broadcast Information Service (FBIS), Radio Free Europe and Radio Liberty (RFE/RL), and the Open Media Research Institute (*OMRI*).
58. Executives won all of the constitutional votes they held—18 out of 18. In the Large-N Data Set the following numbered referendums corresponds to these votes: 27, 31, 36, 37, 41, 42, 45, 58, 60, 61, 65, 66, 78, 83, 85, 86, 87, 141.
59. This number includes referendums from 1990 and 1997.
60. The two Chilean referendums discussed in chapter 2, however, have been associated with conflict. The 1973 proposed vote by Allende may very well have been the proximate cause for the 1973 Coup. An air of violence permeated Chilean society during the 1988 referendum, and Augusto Pinochet would have used violence to delegitimize his referendum loss if the Chilean military had not abandoned him.

Chapter 6   Pros and Cons of Referendums and
Democratic Theory

1. Richard Morin, "The Gloom Boom: Are Voters Really More Cynical Now?" *Washington Post*, Sep. 30, 1990.
2. I consider the "people" in Marx's writings to be the working classes or proletarians.
3. Angela Stint, "What Is To Be Done?" *Washington Post*, Feb. 16, 1992.
4. Alexander, Rubtsov, *Moscow News*, No. 9.
5. FBIS DR, Feb. 20, 1991, p. 56.
6. FBIS DR, Feb. 15, 1991, pp. 36–7.
7. Of course, Russian populations in non-Russian regions and republics were put there deliberately to ensure the assimilation of the population and control from Moscow.
8. See Arrow's Impossibility Theorem and Condorcet's paradox, chapter 2 of Peter Ordeshook. 1986. *Game Theory and Political Theory: An Introduction*, New York: Cambridge University Press.
9. Large states within countries, like California in the United States, also have long track records with direct democracy.
10. This all-or-nothing situation best applies to referendums with only one question. The April 1993 Russian referendums, e.g., offered a spectrum of responses to the voters regarding their opinions of President Yeltsin and the Russian Parliament.

Bibliography

Americas Watch Committee. 1988. *Chile: Human Rights and the Plebiscite.* New York: Americas Watch.

Arriagada, Genaro. 1988. *Pinochet: The Politics Of Power.* Boston: Unwin Hyman.

Arrow, Kenneth J. 1950. "A Difficulty in the Concept of Social Welfare." *Journal of Political Economy* 58: 328–46.

Association Francaise de Science Politique as Cahiers de la Fondation Nationale des Sciences Politiques, *L'Etablissment de la Ve Republique: Le Referendum de septembre et les elections de novembre 1958* (Paris, 1960); *Le Referendum du 8 janvier 1961* (Paris, 1962); *Le Referendum du 8 avril 1962* (Paris, 1969); *Le Referendum d'octobre et les elections de novembre 1962* (Paris, 1965).

Aubert, Jean-François. 1978. "Switzerland." In *Referendums: A Comparative Study of Practice and Theory,* ed. David Butler and Austin Ranney. Washington, DC: The American Enterprise Institute.

Auer, Andreas and Michael Bützer, eds. 2001. *Direct Democracy: The Eastern and Central European Experience.* Burlington: Ashgate.

Baylis, Thomas A. 1996. "Presidents versus Prime Ministers: Shaping Executive Authority in Eastern Europe." *World Politics* 48 (3) (April).

Bendix, Reinhard. 1978. *Kings or People: Power and the Mandate to Rule.* Berkeley: University of California Press.

Berstein, Serge. 1993. *The Republic of de Gaulle, 1958–1969.* New York: Cambridge University Press.

Bertier de Sauvigny, Guillaume de and David H. Pinkney. 1983. *History of France: Revised and Enlarged Edition.* Wheeling, IL: Forum press, Inc.

Biulleten Tsentralnoi izbiratelnoi komissii Rossiiskoi Federatsii, No. 1–, Moskva, Izdvo "Izvestiia," 1993–.

Blainey, Geoffrey. 1973. *The Causes of War.* New York: Free Press.

Boldin, Valery. 1994. *Ten Years that Shook the World: The Gorbachev Era as Witnessed by His Chief of Staff.* New York: Basic Books.

Brady, Henry E. and Cynthia S. Kaplan. 1994. "Eastern Europe and the Former Soviet Union." In *Referendums Around the World: The Growing Use of Direct*

Democracy, ed. David Butler and Austin Ranney. Washington, DC: The American Enterprise Institute.

Bremmer, Ian and Ray Taras. 1997. *New States, New Politics: Building the Post-Soviet Nations*. New York: Cambridge University Press.

Breslauer, George W. 1989. "Evaluating Gorbachev as Leader." *Soviet Economy* 5: 336.

Breslauer, George W. 1982. *Khrushchev and Brezhnev as Leaders*. London: George Allen and Unwin.

Broder, David S. 2000. *Democracy Derailed: Initiative Campaigns and the Power of Money*. New York: Harcourt Inc.

Brown, Archie. 1996. *The Gorbachev Factor*. New York: Oxford University Press.

Brudny, Yitzhak M. 1995. "Ruslan Khasbulatov, Aleksandr Rutskoi, and Intraelite Conflict in Post Communist Russia, 1991–1994." In *Patterns in Post-Soviet Leadership*, ed. Timothy J. Colton and Robert C. Tucker. Oxford: Westview Press.

Burns, James MacGregor. 1978. *Leadership*. New York: Harper & Row.

Butler, David and Austin Ranney, eds. 1994. *Referendums Around the World: The Growing Use of Direct Democracy*. Washington, DC: The American Enterprise Institute.

Butler, David and Austin Ranney, eds. 1978. *Referendums: A Comparative Study of Practice and Theory*. Washington, DC: The American Enterprise Institute.

Cain, Bruce and Pablo T. Spiller. 1991. "The Logic of Initiative Actions." University of California, Berkeley. Typescript.

Center for the Preservation of Contemporary Documentation. 1991. Moscow: Fond 89, perechen' 22, document 81.

Codevilla, Angelo. 1993. "Is Pinochet the Model?" *Foreign Affairs* 72(5): 127–40.

Collie, Melissa P. and Joseph Cooper. 1989. "Multiple Referral and the 'New' Committee System in the House of Representatives." In *Congress Reconsidered*, 4th ed., ed. L. Dodd and B. Oppenheimer. Washington, DC: Congressional Quarterly Press.

Colton, Timothy and Robert C. Tucker. 1995. *Patterns in Post-Soviet Leadership*. Oxford: Westview Press.

Constable, Pamela and Arturo Valenzuela. 1991. *A Nation of Enemies: Chile Under Pinochet*. New York: W. W. Norton & Company, Inc.

Constitution of the Fifth Republic of France.

Cooper, Joseph and David Brady. 1981. "Institutional Context and Leadership Style: The House from Cannon to Rayburn." *American Political Science Review* 75: 411–25.

Cox, Gary W. and Mathew D. McCubbins. 1993. *Legislative Leviathan: Party Government in the House*. Berkeley: University of California Press.

Cronin, Thomas E. 1989. *Direct Democracy: The Politics of Initiative, Referendum, and Recall*. Cambridge, MA: Harvard University Press.

Dahl, Robert A. 1998. *On Democracy*. New Haven: Yale University Press.

Davis, Nathaniel. 1985. *The Last Two Years of Salvador Allende*. Ithaca, NY: Cornell University Press.

Davydov, A. A. 1991. "Vsesoyuznyi referendum—vzglyad sotsiologa." *Sotsiologicheskie issledovaniya*, No. 8, 154.

De Gaulle, Charles. 1970. *Discours et Messages*. Paris: Plon. Quoted in Jean Lacouture. 1991. *De Gaulle: The Ruler 1945–1970*. New York: W. W. Norton & Company and in Serge Berstein. 1993. *The Republic of de Gaulle, 1958–1969*. New York: Cambridge University Press.

Diamond, Larry and Marc F. Plattner, eds. 1996. *The Global Resurgence of Democracy*, 2nd ed. Baltimore: Johns Hopkins University Press.

Downs, Anthony. 1957. *An Economic Theory of Democracy*. New York: Harper & Row.

Easter, Gerald M. 1997. "Preference for Presidentialism: Postcommunist Regime Change in Russia and the NIS." *World Politics* 49(2), (January).

Erikson, Robert S., Gerald C. Wright, and John P. McIver. 1993. *Statehouse Democracy: Public Opinion and Policy in the American States*. Cambridge: Cambridge University Press.

Falcoff, Mark. 1989. *Modern Chile 1970–1989: A Critical History*. New Brunswick, NJ: Transaction Publishers.

Fenno, Richard F. 1973. *Congressmen in Committees*. Boston: Little, Brown.

Fish, M. Steven. 1996. "Russia's Fourth Transition." In *The Global Resurgence of Democracy*, 2nd ed., ed. Larry Diamond and Marc F. Plattner. Baltimore: Johns Hopkins University Press.

Frears, John R. 1991. *Parties and Voters in France*. New York: St. Martin's Press.

Frears, John R. 1977. *Political Parties and Elections in the French Fifth Republic*. New York: St. Martin's Press.

Friedman, Milton. 1982. *Capitalism and Freedom*. Chicago: University of Chicago Press.

Gallagher, Michael and Pier Vincenzo Uleri. 1996. *The Referendum Experience in Europe*. New York: St. Martin's.

Garcés, Joan. 1974. *Allende y la experiencia chilena*. Mexico: Siglo XXI. Quoted in Edy Kaufman. 1988. *Crisis in Allende's Chile: New Perspectives*. New York: Praeger.

Gerber, Elisabeth R. 1999. *The Populist Paradox: Interest Group Influence and the Promise of Direct Legislation*. Princeton: Princeton University Press.

Gerber, Elisabeth R. 1996a. "Legislative Response to the Threat of Popular Initiatives." *American Journal of Political Science*, 40 (1): 99–128.

Gerber, Elisabeth R. 1996b. "Legislatures, Initiatives, and Representation: The Effects of State Legislative Institutions on Policy." *Political Research Quarterly* 49: 2, 263–86.

Goguel, François. 1962. *Le référendum du 8 janvier 1961*. Préf de Jean Touchard. Paris: A. Colin.

Gorbachev, Mikhail S. 1996. *Memoirs*. New York: Doubleday.

Gorbachev, Mikhail S. 1988. *Perestroika: New Thinking for Our Country and the World, New Updated Edition.* New York: Harper & Row, Publishers.

Gutierrez, Raul. *Informe politico a marzo 1989.*

Gwertzman, Bernard and Michael T. Kaufman, eds. 1992. *The Decline and Fall of the Soviet Empire.* New York: Times Books.

Hall, Richard L. 1989. "Committee Decision Making in the Postreform Congress." In *Congress Reconsidered,* 4th ed., ed. L. Dodd and B. Oppenheimer. Washington, DC: Congressional Quarterly Press.

Halperin, Morton H. 1974. *Bureaucratic Politics and Foreign Policy.* Washington: Brookings Institution.

Haskell, John. 2001. *Direct Democracy or Representative Democracy? Dispelling the Populist Myth.* Boulder: Westview Press.

Hayward, Jack, ed. 1993. *De Gaulle to Mitterrand: Presidential Power in France.* New York: New York University Press.

Hayward, Jack. 1969. "Presidential Suicide by Plebiscite: de Gaulle's Exit." *Parliamentary Affairs* 22: 289–319.

Held, David. 1996. *Models of Democracy,* 2nd ed. Stanford: Stanford University Press.

Hill, Ronald J. and Stephen White. 1995. *The Referendum in Communist and Post-Communist Europe—SPP 243.* Glasgow: Centre for the Study of Public Policy, University of Strathclyde.

Hough, Jerry F. 1997. *Democratization and Revolution in the USSR, 1985–1991.* Washington, DC: Brookings Institution Press.

Huntington, Samuel P. 1996. "Democracy's Third Wave." In *The Global Resurgence of Democracy,* 2nd ed., ed. Larry Diamond and Marc F. Plattner. Baltimore: Johns Hopkins University Press.

Huntington, Samuel P. 1968. *Political Order in Changing Societies.* New Haven: Yale University Press.

Institut français de l'opinion publique. 1971. *Les Français et de Gaulle.* Paris: Plon, 228.

Johnson, Paul. 1994. "A World Without Leaders." *Commentary,* July.

Johnston, Richard, Andre Blais, Henry E. Brady, and Jean Crete. 1992. *Letting the People Decide: Dynamics of a Canadian Election.* Stanford: Stanford University Press.

Johnston, Richard et al. 1996. *The Challenge of Direct Democracy: The 1992 Canadian Referendum.* Montreal: McGill-Queen's University Press.

Kaplan, Cynthia S. and Henry E. Brady. 1997. "The Communist Party on the Eve of Collapse." In *The Legacy of the Soviet Bloc,* ed. Jane Shapiro Zacek and Ilpyong J. Kim. Gainesville: University Press of Florida.

Kaufman, Edy. 1988. *Crisis in Allende's Chile: New Perspectives.* New York: Praeger.

Kiewiet, D. Roderick and Mathew D. McCubbins. 1991. *The Logic of Delegation: Congressional Parties and the Appropriations Process.* Chicago: University of Chicago Press.

Król, Marcin. 1996. "Where East Meets West." In *The Global Resurgence of Democracy*, 2nd ed., ed. Larry Diamond and Marc F. Plattner. Baltimore: Johns Hopkins University Press.

Lacouture, Jean. 1991. *De Gaulle: The Ruler 1945–1970*. New York: W. W. Norton & Company.

Lakoff, George. 1987. *Women, Fire, and Dangerous Things: What Categories Reveal about the Mind*. Chicago: The University of Chicago Press.

Lampert, Nicholas. 1990. "Patterns of Participation." In *Developments in Soviet Politics*, ed. Stephen White, Alex Pravda, and Zvi Gitelman. Durham: Duke University Press.

Lapidus, Gail W. 1989. "Gorbachev's Nationalities Problem." *Foreign Affairs* (Fall): 92–108.

Lapidus, Gail W. 1989. "Toward the Emergence of Civil Society in the Soviet Union." In *Politics, Society, and Nationality: Inside Gorbachev's Russia*, ed. Seweryn Bialer. Boulder: Westview Press.

Lee, Eugene C. 1978. "California." In *Referendums: A Comparative Study of Practice and Theory*, ed. David Butler and Austin Ranney. Washington, DC: The American Enterprise Institute.

Linz, Juan J. 1993. "Innovative Leadership in the Transition to Democracy and a New Democracy: The Case of Spain." In *Innovative Leaders in International Politics*, ed. Gabriel Sheffer. Albany: State University of New York Press.

Madison, James. 1788. *The Federalist Papers*, No. 10.

Mathews, David. 1994. *Politics for People: Finding a Responsible Public Voice*. Champaign: University of Illinois Press.

Matlock, Jack F., Jr. 1995. *Autopsy on an Empire: The American Ambassador's Account of the Collapse of the Soviet Union*. New York: Random House.

Mayhew, David R. 1974. *Congress: The Electoral Connection*. New Haven: Yale University Press.

McAuley, Mary. 1997. *Russia's Politics of Uncertainty*. New York: Cambridge University Press.

McFaul, Michael. 1997. *Russia's Presidential Elections: The End of Polarized Politics*. Stanford: Hoover Institution Press.

McFaul, Michael. 1995. "State Power, Institutional Change, and the Politics of Privitization in Russia." *World Politics* 47 (January): 210–43.

McFaul, Michael. 1993. *Post-Communist Politics: Democratic Prospects in Russia and Eastern Europe*. SIS Vol. 15, No. 3 *Creating the Post-Communist Order*. Washington: Center for Strategic & International Studies.

McFaul, Michael and Nikolai Petrov. 1997. *Russia: An Electoral History 1989–96*. Washington, DC: Carnegie Endowment for International Peace.

McFaul, Michael and Nikolai Petrov, eds. 1995. *Previewing Russia's 1995 Parliamentary Elections*. Washington, DC: Carnegie Endowment for International Peace.

Mendelsohn, Matthew and Andrew Parkin, eds. 2001. *Referendum Democracy: Citizens, Elites, and Deliberation in Referendum Campaigns*. New York: Palgrave.

Mill, John Stuart. 1951. *Considerations on Representative Government*. In *Utilitarianism, Liberty, and Representative Government*, ed. H. B. Acton. London: Dent.

Miller, Arthur H., William M. Reisinger, and Vicki L. Hesli. 1996. "Understanding Political Change in Post-Soviet Societies: A Further Commentary on Finifter and Mickiewicz." *American Political Science Review* 90 (1) (March).

Moore, Barrington, Jr. 1966. *Social Origins of Dictatorship and Democracy: Lord and Peasant in the Making of the Modern World*. Boston: Beacon Press.

Morrow, James D. 1994. *Game Theory for Political Scientists*. Princeton: Princeton University Press.

National Democratic Institute for International Affairs. 1988. *Chile's Transition to Democracy: The 1988 Presidential Plebiscite*. Washington, DC: National Democratic Institute for International Affairs.

Nef, J. and Remonda Bensabat. 1989. "Chilean plebiscite: exit Pinochet?" *International Perspectives* 18(1): 18–21.

Nikonov, V. A. and S. A. Kolmakov. 1992. "Zakon o Viborah: Optimalinaia." *Rossiiskii Monitor*, Moscow, Center "INDEM," No. 3 (September).

Nunez-Tome, Leopoldo-M. 1988. "El plebiscito presidencial de 1988." *Politica*, Je 1988: 75–81.

O'Donnell, Guillermo and Phillipe C. Schmitter. 1986. *Transitions from Authoritarian Rule: Tentative Conclusions about Uncertain Democracies*. Baltimore: Johns Hopkins University Press.

O'Neil, Patrick H. 1996. "Revolution from Within: Institutional Analysis, Transitions from Authoritarianism, and the Case of Hungary." *World Politics* 48 (4) (July).

Olson, Mancur, Jr. 1965. *The Logic of Collective Action: Public Goods and the Theory of Groups*. Cambridge, MA: Harvard University Press.

Oppenheim, Lois Hecht. 1993. *Politics in Chile: Democracy, Authoritarianism, and the Search for Development*. Boulder: Westview Press.

Ordeshook, Peter. 1986. *Game Theory and Political Theory: An Introduction*. New York: Cambridge University Press.

Petras, James and Fernando-Ignacio Leiva. 1988. "Chile: The Authoritarian Transition To Electoral Politics; A Critique." *Latin-American-Perspectives* 15: 97–114.

Petrov, N. V. 1992. "Referendum 25 Aprelia 1993 goda: Itogi i Yroki." *Rossiiskii Monitor*, Moscow, Center "INDEM," No. 3 (September).

Pinochet Ugarte, Augusto. 1980. *El Día Decisivo*. Santiago: Andres Bello.

Potichnyj, Peter. 1991. "The Referendum and Presidential Elections in Ukraine." *Canadian Slavonic Papers* 33: 123–38.

Powell, Robert. 1999. *In the Shadow of Power: States and Strategies in International Politics*. Princeton, NJ: Princeton University Press.

Powell, Robert. 1996a. "Bargaining in the Shadow of Power." *Games and Economic Behavior* 15: 255–89.

Powell, Robert. 1996b. "Stability and the Distribution of Power." *World Politics* 48: 239–67.

Price, Roger. 1993. *A Concise History of France.* New York: Cambridge University Press.

Przeworski, Adam and Fernando Limongi. 1997. "Modernization: Theories and Facts." *World Politics* 49(2) (January).

Quilter, Peter A. 1989. "Television in the Chilean Plebiscite of 1988." *Fletcher-Forum-of-World-Affairs* 13 (September): 295–305.

Qvortrup, Mads. 2002. *A Comparative Study of Referendums: Government by the People.* New York: Manchester University Press.

Reddaway, Peter. 1990. "The Quality of Gorbachev's Leadership." *Soviet Economy* 6: 125–40.

Remnick, David. 1997. *Resurrection: The Struggle for a New Russia.* New York: Random House.

Remnick, David. 1994. *Lenin's Tomb: The Last Days of the Soviet Empire.* New York: Vintage Books.

Report-on-the-Americas. 1988. "Pinochet's Plebiscite: Choice With No Options." 22: 13–40

Riker, William H. 1982 [1988]. *Liberalism Against Populism: A Confrontation Between the Theory of Democracy and the Theory of Social Choice.* Prospect Heights, IL: Waveland Press, Inc.

Rohde, David W. 1991. *Parties and Leaders in the Postreform House.* Chicago: University of Chicago Press.

Romer, Thomas and Howard Rosenthal. 1979. "Bureaucrats Versus Voters: On the Political Economy of Resource Allocation by Direct Democracy." *The Quarterly Journal of Economics* (November).

Romer, Thomas and James M. Snyder, Jr. 1994. "An Empirical Investigation of the Dynamics of PAC Contributions." *American Journal of Political Science* 38: 745–69.

Schneider, Cathy Lisa. 1995. *Shantytown Protest in Pinochet's Chile.* Philadelphia: Temple University Press.

Sella, Amnon. 1993. "Gorbachev: The Devolution of Power." In *Innovative Leaders in International Politics,* ed. Gabriel Sheffer. Albany: State University of New York Press.

Setälä, Maija. 1999. *Referendums and Democratic Government: Normative Theory and the Analysis of Institutions.* New York: St. Martin's Press.

Sheehy, Ann. "The March 17 Referendum on Preservation of Union." *Report on the USSR,* Vol. 3, No. 7, February 15, 1991: 5–7.

Sheffer, Gabriel, ed. 1993. *Innovative Leaders in International Politics.* Albany: State University of New York Press.

Sigmund, Paul E. 1977. *The Overthrow of Allende and the Politics of Chile, 1964–1976.* Pittsburgh: University of Pittsburgh Press.

Sinclair, Barbara. 1983. *Majority Leadership in the U.S. House.* Baltimore, MD: Johns Hopkins University Press.

Slater, Wendy. 1993. "No Victors in the Russian Referendum." *Radio Free Europe/Radio Liberty Research Report*, Vol. 2, No. 21, May 21, 1993.

Snidal, Duncan. 1979. "Public Goods, Property Rights, and Political Organizations." *International Studies Quarterly* 23(4): 532–66.

Solzhenitsyn, Aleksandr. 1991. *Rebuilding Russia: Reflections and Tentative Proposals*. New York: Farrar, Straus, and Giroux.

Spooner, Mary Helen. ca. 1994. *Soldiers in a Narrow Land: The Pinochet Regime in Chile*. Berkeley: University of California Press.

Staff of the Commission on Security and Cooperation in Europe. 1994. *Ukraine's Parliamentary Election, March 27, 1994 and April 10, 1994*. Washington, DC: U.S. Government Printing Office.

Staff of the Commission on Security and Cooperation in Europe. 1994. *Russia's Parliamentary Election and Constitutional Referendum: December 12, 1993*. Washington, DC: U.S. Government Printing Office.

Staff of the Commission on Security and Cooperation in Europe. 1993. *Report on the April 25, 1993, Referendum in Russia*. Washington, DC: U.S. Government Printing Office.

Staff of the Commission on Security and Cooperation in Europe. 1991. *Referendum in the Soviet Union: A Compendium of Reports on the March 17, 1991 Referendum on the Future of the U.S.S.R.* Washington, DC: U.S. Government Printing Office.

U.S. Congress. House. Committee on Foreign Affairs. 1988. *Human Rights and the Prospects for Democracy in Chile: Report of a Staff Study Mission to Chile, November 28–December 7, 1987.*

Valenzuela, Arturo and Pamela Constable. 1988. "Plebiscite in Chile: End of the Pinochet Era?" *Current History* 87: 29–33.

Van Atta, Don. 1989. "The USSR as a 'Weak State': Agrarian Origins of Resistance to Perestroika." *World Politics* 42 (October).

Villagran, Fernando. 1988. "Pinochet's Plebiscite: Choice With No Options." *Report-on-the-Americas* 22: 4–20.

von Mettenheim, Kurt. 1997. *Presidential Institutions and Democratic Politics: Comparing Regional and National Contexts*. Baltimore: Johns Hopkins University Press.

Walker, Edward. 1993. "The Politics of Blame and Presidentialism in Russia's New Constitution." *East European Constitutional Review*, 2(4) (Winter).

Walker, Mark Clarence. 1991. "The Political Philosophy of Mikhail Sergeyevich Gorbachev." Undergraduate thesis. Massachusetts Institute of Technology.

Weber, Max. 1978. *Economy and Society*, 2 vols., ed. Guenther Roth and Claus Wittich Berkeley: University of California Press.

Weber, Max. 1964. *Theory of Social and Economic Organization*. New York: The Free Press.

White, Stephen, Richard Rose, and Ian McAllister. 1997. *How Russia Votes*. Chatham, NJ: Chatham House.

White, Stephen, Alex Pravda, and Zvi Gitelman, eds. 1990. *Developments in Soviet Politics*. Durham: Duke University Press.

Williams, Phillip M. 1970. *French Politicians and Elections 1951–1969*. New York: Cambridge University Press.

Williams, Phillip M. 1968. *The French Parliament (1958–1967)*. London: George, Allen and Unwin, Ltd.

Wills, Garry. 1994a. *Certain Trumpets*. New York: Simon & Schuster.

Wills, Garry. 1994b. "What Makes a Good Leader?" *The Atlantic Monthly* (April).

Wright, Vincent. 1978. "France." In *Referendums: A Comparative Study of Practice and Theory*, ed. David Butler and Austin Ranney. Washington, DC: The American Enterprise Institute.

Yeltsin, Boris. 1994. *The Struggle for Russia*. New York: Times Books.

Index

References to figures and tables in **bold**.

Akayev, Askar, 19, 98–103, 104
Alcuin of York, 10, 11
Armenia, 63, **66**
autonomy referendums, 9, 15, 43, 50,
    93, 106–9, 110–6, **111**, **113**
Azerbaijan, 63, **66**, 68

bargaining, *see* elites
Belorus, 63, **66**, 68
Bendix, Reinhard, 10–11

carryover institutions, 7–9, 14, 81, 94
Chile, 43–48
    proposed referendum of 1973,
        43–6, **93**
    referendum of 1988, 43, 46–8, **93**
conflict, *see* violence
constitutional referendums, 9, 43, 93,
    104–6, **111**, 111–13, **113**, 116
counter-referendums, 49–50, 63–66
Crimea, 106–9

De Gaulle, Charles, 12, 13, 19–43, **94**,
    95, 97
democracy
    direct, 4, 101–2, 120, 125–6
    representative, 4, 19, 101–2, 125–6
distribution of power, 13–14, 24–6,
    32–43, 74–5, 101

elites, 3–5, **93**
    elite bargaining, 3–5, 11–13, 74–80

Estonia, **66**
ethnic groups, 15, 50–1, 106–9, 114,
    123–4
executives, 3–5, 19–21, 48, 91–7, **93**,
    104, 110–2, **111**, 121–2

France
    Fourth Republic, 23–4
    referendum by Louis Napoleon, 22
    referendums by Napoleon
        Bonaparte, 22
    referendums in the Fourth
        Republic, 23
    referendum of 1958, 24–6, 48, **93**
    referendum of 1961, 26–8, 48, **93**
    referendum of 1962 April, 28–32,
        48, **93**
    referendum of 1962 October, 32–6,
        48, **93**
    referendum of 1969, 36–43, 48, **93**

Georgia, 63, **66**
Gorbachev, Mikhail, 12, 13–14, 51–61,
    65–71, **94**, 95–6

informal groups, 54–5

Kazakhstan, 63, 65, **66**, 68
Khasbulatov, Ruslan, 13, 73, **76**, 77,
    79, 81, 86–7
Kravchuk, Leonid, 19, 64, 104–5, 106
Kuchma, Leonid, 19, 104, 105–6

Kyrgyzstan, 63, **66**, 67
  referendum of January 1994, 98–100
  referendum of October 1994, 100–3

Latvia, **66**
laws, 131–2
leadership, **94**, 94–7
legislatures, 3–9, 16–17, 19–21, 79–80,
  89–90, 92–4, **93**, 110–12, **111**
legitimacy, 10–13, 56–7, 69, 73, 78,
  118–9
Lithuania, 63, **66**

median voter, 5–6, **6**, 71
military, 43–8, 79, 86–7, 92–3, **93**
Moldova, 63, **66**

nationalism, 71, 114
Nazarbaev, Nursultan, 61, 65
Niyazov, Saparmurad, 61

policy referendums, 9, 111, **111**, **113**,
  113–14, 116
polling, 81–2, 83–4, 99
Pinochet, Augusto, 12, 19, 21–2, 43–7,
  94, 95, 97

rational choice theory, 3
referendums
  boycotts, 63
  categories, 9–10
  definition, 1
  forged, 99–100
  interpretation, 11, 85–6, 100, 123
  "personal" connection to people,
    19–22, 31, 40–2

timing, 11, 45–6, 87–8, 123
  wording, 11, 35, 62, 63, 65, 82–4,
    122–3, 131
  *see also under individual countries and
    regions*
reversion point, 21
Russia, 63–4, **66**, 68
  presidency, 73–4
  referendum of March 1991, 64, **66**,
    67, 68, 74
  referendums of April 1993, 73,
    78–87, **93**, 98
  referendum of December 1993, 73,
    87–9, 98, 101

Soviet Union
  referendum of 1991, 49–51, 52,
    58–71, **93**
spatial models, 5–9, **8**, **76**

Tajikistan, 63, **66**, 68
transitions, 15, 18, 77–8
Turkmenistan, 63, **66**, 68

Ukraine, 63, 64–5, **66**, 67, 104–6
  see also Crimea
Uzbekistan, 63, **66**, 67–8

violence, 14–15, 69–70, 74–5, 79–80,
  86–7, 115–16, 126–31

Yeltsin, Boris, 13, 14, 19, 63–4, 68,
  73–4, **76**, 79, 80–90, **94**, 95,
  96–7, 104

zero-sum game, 2, 4